What People Are Saying about

HOW NOW SHALL WE LIVE?

"A bracing challenge—just what the Christian church needs to hear in the new millennium. A very powerful book."—**The Honorable Jack Kemp**

"How Now Shall We Live? is truly inspiring for those who want to restore to our culture the values that made America great. It reminds us that we must not only defend what we believe, but also inspire others to give witness to the truth alongside us."—**The Honorable Tom DeLay,** Majority Whip, United States House of Representatives

"The singular pleasure that comes from it is its absolute—learned—refusal to give any quarter to the dogged materialists who deny any possibility that there was a creator around the corner. This is a substantial book, but the reader never tires, as one might from a catechistic marathon. The arguments are cogently and readably presented."—**William F. Buckley** in *National Review*

"The newest—and certainly the most important—of Charles Colson's books . . . the essence of this book is that the Christian faith is not just a theory, not just a system, not just a framework. It is an all-consuming way of life, robustly applicable to every minute of every day of the rest of your life."—*World*

"There is something wrong with the historical development of the evangelical mind, . . . a lopsidedness, a prodigious development of one divine gift coupled with the atrophy of another. . . . We know a great deal about saving grace, but next to nothing—though it is one of our doctrines—about common grace. The ambition of Charles Colson and Nancy Pearcey is to do something about this lopsidedness, to strike a blow against the scandal of the evangelical mind. . . . A highly intelligent book, it is not ashamed to speak to ordinary folk."—*First Things*

"How Now Shall We Live? is brilliantly lit by its in-depth and succinct diagnosis of the modern mentality . . . an intelligent and thoroughgoing critique from a Scriptural perspective, of the American/Western culture. . . . The book is a veritable mosaic of precious intellectual gems, artistically designed by Charles Colson and Nancy Pearcey. . . . This book is a virtual 'must' for the thinking Orthodox reader."—*DOXA,* a quarterly review serving the Orthodox Church

"A magnum opus in the best Schaefferian tradition. It is clearly intended to be . . . a handbook for today's Christian. . . . The authors presuppose that Christianity is more than just a religion of personal salvation: it involves a total world-and-life view."—*Christianity Today*

"A very good and much needed book. . . . Colson argues that Christianity isn't a private faith but a public worldview that, for believers, permeates politics, the arts, education, science and culture."—*Insight*

An "elegantly written tutorial on adopting a biblical worldview and the discipline of thinking Christianly."—*Good News*

"I'd like to recommend a book. It's *How Now Shall We Live?* by Charles Colson, the Watergate guy who got religion while in prison. . . . Now I don't agree with everything Colson says, but the importance of the book is that it raises a question every American ought to face and then answer to his or her own satisfaction: What is your world view?"—**Charley Reese,** nationally syndicated columnist.

One of "Ten Books Every Preacher Should Read This Year."—*Preaching*

"Deeply troubled by the lack of biblical literacy within the American Church, this is Colson's heroic effort to enable believers to accept the importance of having a biblical worldview and devoting themselves to adopting such a life perspective. . . . This book provides a wealth of insight into how we may effectively challenge the post-Christian, post-modern culture in which we live."—*The Barna Report*

"Colson and Pearcey aren't talking about influencing business, politics and culture—they want it transformed through a coherent Christian world view. Their book will challenge every Christian leader to make an honest assessment about his or her commitment to use leadership gifts in the new millennium to the cause of Christ."—*Christian Management Report*

"Colson and Pearcey challenge the church to stay on the front lines. Believing that America is on the verge of a great spiritual breakthrough, the authors want to equip readers to show the world that Christianity is a life system that *works* in every area—family relationships, education, science, and popular culture."—*Virtue*

"A radical challenge to all Christians to understand biblical faith as an entire world view, a perspective on all of life. Through inspiring teaching and true stories, Colson discusses how to expose the false views and values of modern culture, how to live more fulfilling and satisfying lives in line with the way God created us to live—and more."—*Youthworker*

[In developing and implementing an organizational learning strategy and integrating it with their organizational practices] "When it came to selecting materials, your *How Now Shall We Live?* was at the top of the list. To our minds this is now the best introduction to a Christian worldview and Christian cultural engagement available in English. At least in our organization, *How Now Shall We Live?* should become an indispensable resource."—*Christian Labour Association of Canada*

1999 Books of the Year—Award of Merit—*Christianity Today*

SCIENCE
AND
EVOLUTION

DEVELOPING
A CHRISTIAN
WORLDVIEW OF

SCIENCE
AND
EVOLUTION

CHARLES
COLSON

AND NANCY PEARCEY

Tyndale House Publishers, Inc.
Wheaton, Illinois

Visit Tyndale's exciting Web site at www.tyndale.com

Science and Evolution

Text copyright © 1999 by Charles Colson. All rights reserved.

Introduction copyright © 2001 by Charles Colson. All rights reserved.

Group study materials copyright © 2001 by Tyndale House Publishers, Inc. All rights reserved.

"How Now Shall We Live?" is a trademark of Tyndale House Publishers, Inc.

Cover photograph of man copyright © 2001 by Ron Chapple/FPG. All rights reserved.

Cover photograph of globe copyright © 2001 By David Greenwood/FPG. All rights reserved.

Charles Colson photo taken by Russ Busby. All rights reserved.

Nancy Pearcey photo copyright © 1999 by Lasting Images. All rights reserved.

Designed by Kelly Bennema

Edited by Lynn Vanderzalm and MaryLynn Layman

The text for this book is composed of chapters 5–14 of *How Now Shall We Live?* by Charles Colson and Nancy Pearcey. The stories in this book are based on facts resulting from extensive research and from interviews with many of the main characters involved. However, some of the secondary characters in the stories are fictionalized or composite characters; any resemblance to real characters is purely coincidental. In addition, events and circumstances may have been rearranged for dramatic purposes.

Unless otherwise indicated, all Scripture quotations are taken from the *Holy Bible,* New International Version®. NIV®. Copyright © 1973, 1978, 1984 by International Bible Society. Used by permission of Zondervan Publishing House. All rights reserved.

Scripture quotations marked "NKJV" are taken from the New King James Version. Copyright © 1979, 1980, 1982 by Thomas Nelson, Inc. Used by permission. All rights reserved.

Scripture quotations marked NASB are taken from the *New American Standard Bible,* © 1960, 1962, 1963, 1968, 1971, 1972, 1973, 1975, 1977 by The Lockman Foundation. Used by permission.

Scripture quotations marked NLT are taken from the *Holy Bible,* New Living Translation, copyright © 1996. Used by permission of Tyndale House Publishers, Inc., Wheaton, Illinois 60189. All rights reserved.

Library of Congress Cataloging-in-Publication Data

Colson, Charles W.
    Science and evolution : developing a Christian worldview of science and evolution / Charles Colson and Nancy Pearcey.
        p. cm.— (Developing a Christian worldview)
    Includes bibliographical references.
    ISBN 0-8423-5583-9 (pbk.)
    1. Creationism. 2. Evolution (Biology)—Religious aspects—Christianity. 3. Apologetics. I. Pearcey, Nancy. II. Title.
    BS651.C623 2001   2001002286

Printed in the United States of America

06   05   04   03   02   01
8   7   6   5   4   3   2   1

CONTENTS

102792

INTRODUCTION:
WHAT IS A WORLDVIEW?

The way we see the world can change the world.

Our choices are shaped by what we believe is real and true, right and wrong, good and beautiful. Our choices are shaped by our worldview.

The term *worldview* may sound abstract or philosophical, a topic discussed by pipe-smoking, tweed-jacketed professors in academic settings. But actually a person's worldview is intensely practical. It is simply the sum total of our beliefs about the world, the "big picture" that directs our daily decisions and actions. And so understanding worldviews is extremely important to how we live—to know how to evaluate everything from the textbooks in our classrooms to the unspoken philosophy that shapes the message we hear on *Oprah*, from the stories and characters shown in contemporary movies to the lyrics in the music we listen to.

The basis for the Christian worldview, of course, is God's revelation in Scripture. Yet sadly, many believers fail to understand that Scripture is intended to be the basis for all of life. In the past centuries, the secular world asserted a dichotomy between science and religion, between fact and value, between objective knowledge and subjective feeling. As a result, Christians often think in terms of the same false dichotomy, allowing our belief system to be reduced to little more than private feelings and experience, divorced from objective facts.

Evangelicals have been particularly vulnerable to this narrow view because of our emphasis on personal commitment. On one

hand, this has been the movement's greatest strength, bringing
millions to a relationship with Christ. Somewhere in most of our
spiritual journeys is a sawdust trail, as there certainly is in mine.
I remember as vividly as if it were yesterday that sultry summer
night in 1973, in the midst of the Watergate scandal, when I, a
former marine captain—often called the "toughest of the Nixon
tough guys," the "White House hatchet man"—broke down in
tears and called out to God.[1] Apart from that encounter with
Christ and assurances of his forgiveness, I would have suffocated
in the stench of my own sin. My soul would never have found rest.

But this emphasis on a personal relationship can also be evangelicalism's greatest weakness because it may prevent us from
seeing God's plan for us beyond personal salvation. Genuine
Christianity is more than a relationship with Jesus as expressed
in personal piety, church attendance, Bible study, and works of
charity. It is more than discipleship, more than believing a system
of doctrines about God. Genuine Christianity is a way of seeing
and comprehending *all* reality.

It is a worldview.

Understanding Christianity as a total life system is absolutely
essential, for two reasons. First, it enables us to make sense of the
world we live in and thus order our lives more rationally. Second,
it enables us to understand forces hostile to our faith, equipping us
to evangelize and to defend Christian truth as God's instruments
for transforming culture.

MORAL ORDER

Because the world was created by an intelligent being rather than
by chance, it has an intelligible order. As Abraham Kuyper, the
great nineteenth-century theologian who served as prime minister
of Holland, wrote, "All created life necessarily bears in itself a law
for its existence, instituted by God Himself."[2] The only way to live

a rational and healthy life is to ascertain the nature of these divine laws and ordinances and then to use them as the basis for how we should live. We tend to understand this principle very well when it comes to the physical order. We know that certain laws exist in the physical world and that if we defy those laws, we pay a steep price. Ignoring the law of gravity can have very unpleasant consequences if we happen to be walking off the edge of a cliff. To live in defiance of known physical laws is the height of folly.

But it is no different with the moral laws prescribing human behavior. Just as certain physical actions produce predictable reactions, so certain moral behavior produces predictable consequences. Hollywood may portray adultery as glamorous, but it invariably produces anger, jealousy, broken relationships, even violence. Defiance of moral laws may even lead to death, whether it is the speeding drunk who kills a mother on her way to the store or the drug addict who contracts and spreads AIDS. No transgression of moral law is without painful consequences.

If we want to live healthy, well-balanced lives, we had better know the laws and ordinances by which God has structured creation. And because these are the laws of our own inner nature, Kuyper notes, we will experience them not as oppressive external constraints but as "a guide through the desert," guaranteeing our safety.³

This understanding of life's laws is what Scripture calls wisdom. "Wisdom in Scripture is, broadly speaking, the knowledge of God's world and the knack of fitting oneself into it," says Cornelius Plantinga Jr., president of Calvin Theological Seminary.⁴ A wise person is one who knows the boundaries and limits, the laws and rhythms and seasons of the created order, both in the physical and the social world. "To be wise is to know reality and then accommodate yourself to it."⁵ By contrast, those who refuse to accommodate to the laws of life are not only immoral but also foolish, no matter how well educated they may be. They fail to recognize the structure of creation and are constantly at odds with reality: "Folly is a stubborn swimming against the stream of the universe . . . spitting into the wind . . . coloring outside the lines."[6]

Precisely. To deny God is to blind ourselves to reality, and the inevitable consequence is that we will bump up against reality in painful ways, just as a blindfolded driver will crash into other drivers or run off the road. We make the bold claim that serious Christians actually live happier, more fulfilled, more productive lives by almost every measure. (Studies are beginning to bear this out.) This simply makes sense. Someone who accepts the contours and limits of the physical and moral order doesn't engage in folly—whether stepping off a cliff or committing adultery or driving drunk.

THE REAL CULTURE WAR

Our calling is not only to order our own lives by divine principles but also to engage the world. We are to fulfill both the *great commission* and the *cultural commission.* We are commanded both to preach the Good News and to bring all things into submission to God's order, by defending and living out God's truth in the unique historical and cultural conditions of our age.

To engage the world, however, requires that we understand the great ideas that compete for people's minds and hearts. Philosopher Richard Weaver has it right in the title of his well-known book: *Ideas Have Consequences.*[7] It is the great ideas that inform the mind, fire the imagination, move the heart, and shape a culture. History is little more than the recording of the rise and fall of the great ideas—the worldviews—that form our values and move us to act.

A debilitating weakness in modern evangelicalism is that we've been fighting cultural skirmishes on all sides without knowing what the war itself is about. We have not identified the worldviews that lie at the root of cultural conflict—and this ignorance dooms our best efforts.

The culture war is not just about abortion, homosexual rights, or the decline of public education. These are only the skirmishes. The real war is a cosmic struggle between worldviews—between the Christian worldview and the various secular and spiritual worldviews arrayed against it. This is what we must understand if we are going to be effective both in evangelizing our world today and in transforming it to reflect the wisdom of the Creator.

WORLDVIEWS IN CONFLICT

The world is divided not so much by geographic boundaries as by religious and cultural traditions, by people's most deeply held beliefs—by worldviews. So argued the distinguished Harvard scholar Samuel Huntington in a celebrated article a few years ago.[8] And Christians would agree. Because we are religious creatures, our lives are defined by our ultimate beliefs more sharply than by any other factor. The drama of history is played out along the frontiers of great belief systems as they ebb and flow.

But if this is so, what does it tell us about the divisions in the world today? Where is the clash of civilizations most bitter?

Huntington predicted a clash between the worldviews of three major traditional civilizations: the Western world, the Islamic world, and the Confucian East. But one of his former students, political scientist James Kurth, took issue with him, contending that the most significant clash would be within Western civilization itself—between those who adhere to a Judeo-Christian framework and those who favor postmodernism and multiculturalism.[9]

I believe Kurth is right. And the reason this conflict within Western culture is so significant is that Western culture may soon dominate the globe. Information technology is rapidly crossing traditional barriers of geography and national boundaries. The fall of the Iron Curtain has opened a large area of the world to Western ideas. Asian and Islamic societies find they cannot insulate themselves from the influx of Western books, movies, and television programs. In Singapore, I met with a Christian cabinet minister who lamented that because Asians associate the West with Christianity, the flood of smut from the West is making his Christian witness difficult. Across the globe, people are complaining about what one French politician described as a "U.S. cultural invasion."[10]

As a result, people around the world are wrestling with the same questions that we face in the States. In Africa, one of the continent's most respected Christian leaders asked for permission to reprint transcripts of my radio program, *BreakPoint.* Though the program is targeted at an American audience, he found that the subjects are the same as those he is dealing with in Africa. Another African Christian leader told me that Western notions of multiculturalism are being used to justify tribalism, and the local church is baffled over how to counter the divisive force. As people in Pakistan get on-line with people in Pennsylvania, America's culture war is increasingly spilling over into other nations.

The sobering conclusion is that our own effectiveness in defending and contending for truth has repercussions across the entire globe. American Christians had better get serious about understanding biblical faith as a comprehensive worldview and showing how it stands up to the challenges of our age.

The three books in this "Developing a Christian Worldview" study series—based on the book *How Now Shall We Live?*—are designed to help you do just that.

Christians must understand the clash of worldviews that is changing the face of society and the world. And we must stand ready to respond as people grow disillusioned with false beliefs and values, and as they begin to seek real answers. We must know not only what our worldview is and why we believe it but also how to defend it. We must also have some understanding of the opposing worldviews and why people believe them. Only then can we present the gospel in language that can be understood. Only then can we defend truth in a way that is winsome and persuasive.

Where did we come from? The question of beginnings is the origin of every important question a person asks. So this book begins where it ought to begin—in the beginning.

HOW TO USE THIS BOOK

This first book in the three-part "Developing a Christian Worldview" series looks at the first worldview question: *Where did we come from, and who are we?* As we discuss and defend our faith, we need to be equipped to counter the prevailing notion that our universe and world are here by chance and that we humans just happened to evolve from amoebas.

This book lays out evidence that our world and its inhabitants are the result of the designing hand of a personal Creator. But it doesn't stop there. As it argues for a creationist worldview, it lays out reasoned arguments showing the flaws in and implications of the naturalist worldview.

To help you understand, assimilate, and remember the material in these chapters, we've incorporated questions and activities for a five-session group study. Small-group study is one of the most dynamic ways we as Christians can learn together and support each other, not only in exploring our worldview, but also in articulating our beliefs in ways that make sense to people who hold opposing worldviews. At the moment, you may not feel qualified or confident enough to speak out about your worldview, but we hope that your group experience will equip you to become an effective communicator of the truth.

PRACTICAL TIPS

At the beginning of each chapter, you'll find questions to help you focus on key points as you read. We suggest that you highlight or underline as you read, marking points you want to remember and points you want to discuss and clarify with your group. In the text of some chapters, key phrases are already underlined to facilitate reading and discussion.

Each study session covers the material in two chapters. At the end of each session-segment you'll find discussion questions. Each set of questions reviews and reinforces the chapter's content. It also draws you to a brief passage of Scripture relevant to the chapter content and/or complementary worldview issues.

We've left some blank space after each question, allowing you to jot notes, but with no clear expectation that you will write down exhaustive answers before you get to the group gathering. The emphasis in this guide is on discussion and group dynamics.

Note that sessions 2 and 3 call for a leader to provide "props" to facilitate discussion. These object lessons and group activities are not simply entertaining time fillers; they are meant to help solidify the truth in your experience. All of us learn and remember things better when we experience them than when we merely hear or read about them. These activities may well trigger the piece of information or reasoned argument that you may need to recall in a later conversation with a skeptic.

This is true also with the suggested role-play activites at the end of each study session. We suggest you commit ten minutes of each session to this role-play activity, in which group members practice presenting to a non-Christian what they've learned in this book. Role plays should not be set up in a manner that traumatizes anyone. The goal is encouragement, not intimidation. See further role-play guidelines and instructions in session 1. Role plays can be set up in groups of two or three, or they can be acted out in front of the whole group.

Each session ends with a closing summary question. We suggest that each person in the group verbalize a one-sentence recap: "The one thing that I want to remember from what I read (or heard or did) in this session is . . ."

HAVING AN IMPACT

We trust that this book will provide your group with a forum for lively discussion, a springboard for action, and a tool for accountability. We encourage you to wrestle with ideas presented in the book. Even if you disagree on some points, we're confident that you will come to a deeper understanding of your worldview. Most of all we hope that you are moved to act, to map out goals and strategies for becoming God's redeeming force in this new millennium.

This book is merely a beginning point for you to explore and pursue the truth of what it means to live out a Christian worldview. Take a serious look at the list of resources in the recommended reading section at the end of the book. Choose several titles to deepen your understanding of specific topics that interest you.

We recommend that you continue your study with the two remaining books in this three-part series: *The Problem of Evil* (six sessions) and *The Christian in Today's Culture* (six sessions).

IS NATURE GOD?
IS SCIENCE RELIGION?

DAVE AND KATY'S
METAPHYSICAL ADVENTURE

As you read, keep the following questions in mind:
What shocking realization did Dave Mulholland make
about . . .

- the place of God in the scientific worldview?
- Katy's view of religion in relation to science?
- Dave's ability to talk with his daughter about the biblical
  perspectives of what they heard and saw?

By day four, the last day of their once-in-a-lifetime trip
together, Dave Mulholland and his fifteen-year-old daughter,
Katy, had memorized the turnoffs along Disney World Drive:
Pleasure Island, River Country, Discovery Island, Disney MGM
Studios, and the Magic Kingdom itself. Today they were pressing
on to Epcot Center to have "a look at the future," as the brochure
advertised.[1]

Disney World Drive itself was as broad as Interstate 4, Dave
marveled, with its own castle-marked, fireworks-bursting signs. It
was like entering a foreign but familiar country. The idea behind
the trip had been for Dave to draw closer to his daughter, to get
behind the emotional walls she had thrown up over the past year.
And in their wanderings through this Luxembourg of the fantas-
tic, he had felt he was reconnecting with her. Until today. It was

Sunday, and Dave had irritated Katy by insisting that they attend church. Now his daughter's stiff silence made him hyperaware of the rental car's four-cylinder, sewing-machine whine.

Suddenly Katy broke her silence. "You think we really saw as much of Disney World as we wanted?" she asked, with just a hint of petulance. "The lines might not be as long today for The Haunted House."

"I want to see Epcot Center," Dave said. "I've heard you have to spend most of the day there to do it justice."

"Dad, *I* told you that this morning." She sighed extravagantly, crossed her arms, and wedged herself back against the door. David knew she was making a show of pouting. And he knew why.

"Look, Katy, the worship service took only an hour. We're still going to be there when the gates open."

She looked pointedly out the window. "Most people just skip church on vacation, Dad. I wanted to sleep in."

Their resort had offered an ecumenical service, and listening to the sentimental, candy-cane sermon, Dave had grimaced inwardly, even feeling a bit guilty for having dragged his daughter out of bed for *this*. But he had reminded himself that at least he was making a testimony about putting first things first. They had gone to church! Now he realized that his great idea had only reinjected much of the tension they had come here to smooth away.

He turned into the exit for Epcot Center and headed for the parking lot.

"Okay," Katy said, picking up her line of argument, "but if this stinks, can we bail? We can just take the monorail over and—"

"If it stinks, we'll be sure to stay until nightfall," Dave teased. "Because personally, you know, I'm down here to have as *bad* a time as possible. I'm really hoping this Epcot thing is *excruciating*."

"Oh, Dad," she groaned. But he sensed some of her anger dissipating.

He paid for their parking ticket and turned back to her. "You know, hon, this is probably the last spring break you'll have time for your male parental unit. I'm glad you wanted to come. Let's have a good day, okay?"

Before he had finished parking, he heard her seat belt unlatch. She leaned across the console and kissed his cheek. "It's been the best," she said.

Kids' moods turn on a dime, Dave thought. *Thank you, Lord.*

"Let's go, then," he said.

The great globe of AT&T's "Spaceship Earth," Epcot's symbol, loomed ahead, but the waiting lines were already filled with people. Dave and Katy had learned to hit second-choice rides or exhibits first; at the start of the day, most visitors were determined to check the big ones off their lists. So the two of them made their way to "The Living Seas."

The exhibit was housed in a building whose curvilinear design evoked waves upon a shore. Inside a blue-green room with low lighting were exhibits of antiquated diving gear and photos of early submarines and diving pools. Dave and Katy hurried through the display, urged forward by an omnipresent recorded voice inviting them to enter a theater where they would witness the birth of the seas.

In the semicircular theater they took their seats, and as they waited for the program to begin, Dave glanced proudly at his daughter. Her pretty, girlish face was acquiring new touches of a more dramatic, womanly beauty, but underneath, he knew, was still a confused mixture of fear and bravado.

Dave and his wife, Claudia, had sensed that Katy was in trouble. It wasn't only the marijuana they had found in her purse, though that in itself had sent them reeling. Worse, they felt they were losing her to a secular world smugly satisfied with itself and deeply hostile to their own. And what stabbed most deeply was that Katy herself was becoming more and more antagonistic to their religious beliefs, to the point where she resisted any involvement in the church's high school group and the Sunday worship services. This from a girl who at age nine had responded to an altar call and given her life to Jesus with free-flowing tears of joy.

THE MAGIC OF EPCOT CENTER

The theater darkened, and Dave's attention was drawn to a man with a handheld mike. "Ocean exploration has come a long way," the man intoned. "But how did the ocean form? When did it form? The answers to those and many other questions are about to surface in a dramatic film simply titled, 'The Sea.' "

With a wave of sound, screens lit up all around, and the audience was surrounded by vivid images. First, the dark eeriness of outer space, suddenly punctuated by countless white spots of brilliance, while a voice invited the audience to imagine a place "somewhere in the endless reaches of the universe, on the other edge of the galaxy of a hundred-thousand-million suns." In this tiny corner of the universe, the mesmerizing voice went on, "deep within the cluster of slowly forming planets," is "a small sphere of just the right size," a sphere "just the right distance from its mother star."

The right size and the right distance for what? Dave was caught up by the spectacular sights unfolding before his eyes, but something pricked his attention in those words. *Just right for life, I suppose,* he thought. Though of course Earth didn't just *happen* to have the right conditions for life; God made it that way, as his faith had taught him. He wondered whether Disney would give even a token nod to the Creator behind it all.

But Dave had little time for reflection. Action was erupting on the huge screen again, where the molten Earth was being shown as a young planet, slowly cooling. It spawned thousands of volcanoes, spewing out gases and steam until the planet was swathed in clouds. The roar of the great eruptions shook the entire room.

Finally, the recorded voice broke in again: "And then the clouds of gas and steam condense and rain upon the planet." Dave heard a sudden, loud rush of rain, so realistic he thought it was pelting the roof of the theater. "Rain and rain and rain," the voice continued, more intensely now. "A deluge!" Torrents of water washed down bare slopes of the lifeless planet. Finally, the seas themselves were born, green waters foaming and churning; and here, the voice said, began the greatest mystery of the universe: life itself. From the play of chemicals in the primeval ocean arose "tiny, single-celled plants that captured the energy of the sun," producing the oxygen required for the more advanced organisms to evolve.

Once again Dave was strangely uneasy. Like the science programs he had watched on television, this one made it sound as if God had nothing to do with any of this, that nature by itself had the power to create the universe and the wonders of life on Earth.

Dave hazarded a sidelong glance at Katy to see if she was at all troubled. But her eyes were fastened to the screen, her uplifted face entranced. And suddenly it struck him that she had no reason to be troubled because she had been hearing the message of evolution all her life from textbooks, teachers, and TV science programs.

When the film ended, they were ushered into "hydrolators," escalator-type contraptions that plunged down to another set of exhibits. There, Katy was delighted with the gigantic aquarium, where divers were training dolphins to communicate with humans. But Dave remained haunted by the image of blue-green seas generating primeval forms of life. Maybe this was one reason for the barrier that had grown up between him and Katy. Was she so inundated with images of a universe without any need for God that she was questioning her faith? Was her rebellion against him and her mother coming from deeper doubts about whether the Bible was true?

When they emerged from "The Living Seas" exhibit, Dave

resorted to humor to break through his obsessive thoughts. He looped Katy's arm through his and strutted like Rex Harrison playing Doctor Dolittle as he sang "If I Could Talk to the Animals."

"*Doctor Dolittle* wasn't a Disney film, Dad," Katy said.

"I don't care. Sing with me."

She was game, and they staged their own little parade, zigzagging down the asphalt, singing under their breath at first and then louder as several passersby offered mock applause.

As they broke apart and stood for a moment laughing, Dave thought of Katy's childhood, when he had called her Miss Disney. During grammar school she had sported Goofy sweatshirts and carried her Minnie Mouse lunch box, even when her friends had moved on to the Ninja Turtles. All of which had led to this moment, for Katy had always longed to come to Disney World, and that almost forgotten wish had resurfaced in Dave's and Claudia's minds as they groped for a way to make her feel special.

Shaking off these memories, Dave steered her toward "The Universe of Energy," with its towering topiary in the shape of a dinosaur. They settled quickly into seats in a large movie theater, where Bill-Nye-the-Science-Guy was soon taking them on an imaginary tour of the history of energy. He started at the ultimate beginning—pointing to a spot where the universe was about to come into existence through the big bang. A spot of light expanded into a thunderous crashing flood as stars exploded and galaxies formed.

Once again, niggling questions began whispering in Dave's mind: What was there *before* the big bang? And how were all the millions of people who trooped through Epcot every year affected when they saw the history of the universe retold in completely natural terms, as if God were irrelevant and unnecessary? More important, what impact was it having on his own daughter?

Just then Katy gasped as the theater seats began to move under them, transforming sections of seating into a thrill-ride mini-train. Bill Nye had transported them to the age of the dinosaurs, explaining that fossil fuels had come from this era millions of years ago in Earth's history. Then a giant comet crashed into the earth, raising a global dust cloud, and the age of the dinosaurs was over.

The moveable seats carried them along to another era, featuring a mock celestial media station with reporters describing a "major upset," the victory of mammals over the dinosaurs in the survival of the fittest. Suddenly another reporter broke in with a news update about the Ice Age, explaining the need for creatures to evolve thick skins and heavy wool coats. That was followed in quick succession by another reporter, who had scooped a story about the glaciers of the Ice Age retreating to the polar circles, making conditions favorable for the emergence of a "whole new kind of creature."

What kind of creature? "Our early ancestors," Bill Nye announced—a creature that screamed like an ape as it kindled a fire.

Dave winced. There it was again—the notion that human beings emerged from a long line of evolutionary forebears through survival of the fittest. No place for the God of the Bible. Just creatures emerging from the slime by chance, as if natural selection were our creator.

The rest of the exhibit covered the various types of energy resources—solar, wind, nuclear, coal, and petroleum—until finally, the trainlike auditorium seats reassembled themselves into a theater.

Relieved that it was over, Dave said, "Let's get lunch."

As he and Katy sat at an outdoor table and munched on their sandwiches, Dave resorted to commenting on the weather. "Sure seems hotter today." But that wasn't what he really wanted to say. Time was running out for the heart-to-heart talk he had planned

to have with Katy on this trip, yet he didn't know how to launch
it. The heat seemed to sizzle into his emotions. He knew the only
way was to force himself simply to plunge in.

"I told you I wanted to have at least one serious talk before we
go back. Remember?" He paused briefly. "How about now?"

Katy looked wary. "Are you and Mom still worried about the
purse thing?"

"That wasn't good."

"Come on, Dad. You didn't have to bring me down here to
convince me not to do marijuana. I only tried it once."

Dave fiddled with his diet Coke. "I worry about *why* you did
it," he said finally.

"You and Mom don't trust me. You act as if I'm ten years old.
You have no idea. . . . You should see how some of my friends
act."

"Oh, I have some idea. I won't bore you with tales of my years
in high school, but I do remember what it was like."

"Could we just get back to being on vacation here? It's almost
over." Katy tilted her head back and pursed her lips.

"I don't know how to explain exactly why I'm worried, Katy.
You *are* a good kid. But I am worried."

"That's your job as a parent, isn't it? And I mean, you are very,
very good at it. But it's okay, Dad." She grinned at him. She could
win him in an instant.

Suddenly, Dave lost all sense of where he wanted this conversation to go. He had to admit that he had seen none of the typical
symptoms of drug use in Katy. No, it wasn't the marijuana episode
he was really concerned about. It was something else that had been
worrying him, and it had been brought into focus at Epcot. He was
concerned most of all about the state of Katy's spiritual life.

After they left the restaurant, they circled around a lagoon and
came to the Norway exhibit, which included a tall, medieval-
looking wooden structure shingled in elaborate layers and appear-

ing strangely out of place in this Land of the Future. Dave grabbed Katy's hand and headed inside. There they were greeted by recorded music, not the usual blare but gentle strains of hymns. The interior was tiny and dark, the light drifting in from openings high up in the steeply sloped ceiling. A placard indicated that the building was a _stave kirke,_ a reproduction of Norway's famous twelfth-century wooden churches. Photos of genuine stave churches lined the walls. In one glass case lay an elaborately worked gold crucifix with Christ robed in blue.

The exhibit was intended as a historical artifact, a museum piece of ancient history. But Dave lingered, suddenly aware of an ethereal quality permeating the dim light, a subtle memory of the days when Christian faith was robust, even heroic.

Katy began fidgeting. "Come on, let's go," she whispered. "There's nothing here."

"Nothing?" Dave asked, without turning around.

"No rides or anything. Let's go."

"In a minute."

Katy snorted and stalked outside. Dave murmured a quick prayer and followed her. But his serious mood was hard to break. As he stopped at a vendor and bought some ice cream and then headed for a nearby bench, he could tell that Katy sensed the change in his mood and knew she could no longer put off "the big talk."

IS IT TRUE?

"So why don't you want to go to church with us anymore?" he said, deciding to jump in with both feet. "What have you got against Christianity?"

Katy turned her head aside. "I don't have anything against it."

"You act as if you're going to die every time we get near anything that has to do with it. You did in there just now."

"Dad, do we have to talk about this? I thought we were just supposed to be here—"

"No," he interrupted, "we aren't *just* supposed to be here on vacation. Your mom and I planned this so that you and I could have some time to talk. That's the hidden agenda. So let's have that talk before we get off this park bench."

Katy attacked her ice cream, her eyes fixed on the dish.

"Look, Katy, your whole attitude toward spiritual things has changed. I want to know what you're thinking."

She took a long breath, then said, "It's just that I don't want to be so different. And I don't have to be," she added in a rush. "I can be a good person without believing the things you believe."

"Different from what?"

"Different from *everybody.*" She waved her hands as if to take in everyone at Disney World. "Hardly anybody believes what you and Mom believe. I have lots of friends who are good people, and they aren't religious."

Katy's words were like barbs piercing his heart, but at least she was talking, at least she was finally opening up to him.

"I don't think it's a question of what anyone *believes,*" Dave said after a painful pause. "Not even what Mom and I believe. It's a question of what's *true.*"

"How does anyone know what's really true?"

"A lot of people think *they* know what's true. We just spent the day going to exhibits where a whole bunch of ideas were presented as true."

"That's science, Dad," Katy said patiently, as if teaching a child. "Science is things that are proved."

"Most of it was more like philosophy, Katy."

"No, it wasn't."

"Yes, it was. Most of the exhibits here share one version of the truth, even when they're talking about different things. It's a story more than anything, and it goes like this: By chance the universe came into existence, by chance Earth was just right for life to exist, by chance life developed into birds and bees and butterflies, by chance human beings came along, and by chance human beings turned out to be so smart that all the world's problems will someday succumb to our technological prowess. End of story. Hallelujah, amen."

"But scientists can prove all that, Dad. No one can know for sure about God."

"Come on, how can anyone 'prove' that the universe came about by chance? Everything I know about the universe, including my incredibly beautiful daughter, indicates to me that Somebody designed it. Created it." All the questions that had been eating at Dave's mind from the time they entered "The Living Seas" were finally taking shape.

"My biology teacher says . . . he says that's our ego talking. People want to believe they're important, so they invent religion. They invent the idea of a God who created them so they'll feel better."

"You really think life came about by chance?"

"It's chemicals. It's all chemicals. We saw how it happened in 'The Living Seas' exhibit. Volcanoes erupting, then the ocean, then chemicals coming together. Scientists have done it in a test tube. I read about it in my science book. I even saw a photo of this thing with glass tubes and electrical sparks and then, you know, molecules came out."

Katy flopped back against the bench, and Dave put his head in his hands. So that was it. She had been so indoctrinated with a secular view of the world, a view backed by the prestige of "science," that Christianity no longer made sense to her. He saw it now. But what could he say to make her change her mind?

"I just can't believe this beautiful world came about by chance." He said it again, more out of desperation than out of any hope that it would make a difference.

"If what you believe is true, Dad, then how come no one else believes it? Listen, last semester in English class we saw a movie called *Inherit the Wind,* and you could see that all the scientists are on the side of Darwin. Christians just close their minds to the facts of science."

Dave sucked in his breath. He felt as if he had been hit in the chest. It made him angry. "Come on, Katy. You know we didn't come from the monkeys." It was a pretty weak response, but it was the best he could muster on the spur of the moment.

Katy looked away without answering.

In despair, Dave realized that he didn't even know how to begin tackling this subject with his daughter. He knew very little about Darwin or evolution. All he really knew—what he felt instinctively—was that if you dismissed God as the Creator, then the whole foundation of faith dissolved. He decided to take a different tack.

"When you went forward in church and became a Christian, Katy . . . doesn't that mean anything to you anymore?" he asked.

Katy bit her knuckle. "I've thought about that—a lot. But how can you trust how you feel in those situations? I mean, I get emotional when I'm watching a movie, and *that's* not real."

"Katy, the two are hardly the same. Giving your life to Christ and . . . and watching a movie."

"All I know is, you and Mom expect me to believe what you believe. If I go to church and pretend to be happy about it, we'll get along. If I don't, you get all serious and make everyone miserable. Just like this trip. It's as if you're blackmailing me."

"Katy, I . . ."

"Do you really love *me,* Dad? The Katy you're talking to right now? Because this is the real me. I'm not the little girl you have in your head."

"Wait a minute. Don't I have a right to disagree with your ideas without you accusing me of not loving you? Who's doing the blackmailing here?"

"They're not just *my* ideas, Dad. They're what I learned in school. They're what everyone believes—even what we saw in the exhibits today. And you can't argue with that."

On that point, she was right, Dave thought grimly. He couldn't argue with *that,* because he didn't know how to begin to counter what she was saying. His daughter seemed to be throwing away her faith, and he had no idea how to stop her. But what he said next came out of a place much deeper than his own frustration and helplessness.

"I'll find out."

"What?"

"I'll find out how to argue with it. I'll find out why the story we heard here today is wrong."

She rolled her eyes scornfully. "Oh come—"

"Or I'll give up my faith, too," he concluded.

She started, as if he had slapped her. Then suddenly she dropped her mock sophistication. "Oh Dad, I don't want . . . you know, *everything* to change."

"But *everything* is at stake here, Katy. That's what you've got to realize. Everything is at stake. Look, if Christianity is true, then it's not my belief or your mother's belief. It's the truth about *reality,* about what is ultimately real. And somehow I am going to find the facts that will show you it's true."

The chief aim of all investigations
of the external world should be to
discover the rational order and
harmony which has been imposed
on it by God. JOHANNES KEPLER

SHATTERING THE GRID

As you read, keep the following questions in mind:

- What is the fundamental assumption of naturalism?
  What makes this a faith-based assumption?

- In what ways did Carl Sagan's *Cosmos* attempt to provide
  a substitute for the Christian religion?

- In talking to others, how can we break the stereotype of
  Christians being ignorant?

- What is the starting point of the Christian worldview?

What hit Dave Mulholland hard in the days that followed
his vacation with Katy was the realization that his daughter had
soaked up a way of thinking that was totally contrary to all he and
Claudia had taught her. And he had discovered this at Disney
World, of all places, where each year more than forty million
people visit, waiting in line to be thrilled, dazzled, and educated.
Many families scrimp all year so they can afford to take their kids
to this Magic Kingdom, this great American icon.

And for what? Dave asked himself grimly. To experience this
paean to secularism, this altar to the power of human ingenuity
and technology?

But at least he now understood what had happened to his
daughter. She had absorbed the idea that science is the source of
truth, while religion is merely subjective opinion, something we
tolerate for those weak enough to need that kind of comfort. And

for the first time, he realized that he had been foolishly overconfident. He had allowed his daughter to be exposed to these ideas in school, on television, and in her books without ever bothering to teach her how to respond.

Perhaps this was not surprising. Dave's own generation had not had to weather such pervasive challenges to Christian faith. For them, religion had been respected, part of the establishment. Dave had never experienced the anguish of doubt. He had always been satisfied with just going to church and holding a set of beliefs that made sense of life.

But now everything had changed. Now he needed to defend what he believed. For his daughter's sake, if not for his own.

"These are not just *my* ideas, Dad," Katy had argued that day at Disney World. "They're what I learned in school. They're what everyone believes."

IS NATURE OUR CREATOR?

Katy was right. The dominant view in our culture today is radically one-dimensional: that this life is all there is, and nature is all we need to explain everything that exists. This is, at heart, the philosophy of naturalism, and not only has it permeated the classroom curriculum, but it has also been expressed widely in popular culture, from Disney World to television nature shows to children's books.

FOUNDATIONAL PREMISES OF NATURALISM

Every worldview has to begin somewhere, has to begin with a theory of how the universe began. Naturalism begins with the fundamental assumption that the forces of nature alone are adequate to explain everything that exists. Whereas the Bible says, "In the beginning God created the heavens and the earth" (Gen. 1:1), naturalists say that in the beginning were the particles, along with

blind, purposeless natural laws. That nature created the universe
out of nothing, through a quantum fluctuation. That nature
formed our planet, with its unique ability to support life. That
nature drew together the chemicals that formed the first living
cell. And naturalism says that nature acted through Darwinian
mechanisms to evolve complex life-forms and, finally, human
beings, with the marvels of consciousness and intelligence.

Naturalistic scientists try to give the impression that they are
fair-minded and objective, implying that religious people are subjective and biased in favor of their personal beliefs. But this is a
ruse, for naturalism is as much a philosophy, a worldview, a personal belief system as any religion is.

Naturalism begins with premises that cannot be tested empiri-
cally, such as the assumption that nature is "all that is or ever was
or ever will be," to use a line from the late Carl Sagan's popular
science program *Cosmos*. This is not a scientific statement, for
there is no conceivable way it could be tested. It is a philosophy.
And as we will see, it is the philosophy that supports the entire
evolutionary enterprise, from its assertions about the beginning of
the universe to the beginning of life to the appearance of complex
life-forms.

As much as anyone else, it was Sagan who popularized the naturalistic worldview and entrenched it firmly in the mind of the
average American. The dark hair swept to one side, the Colgate
smile, the telegenic personality—it all added up to a powerful
influence on the millions of viewers who tuned in to his PBS program *Cosmos*. Week after week, he brought stunning images of
exploding stars and sprawling nebulae into homes and classrooms
across the nation.

Religious Fervor

But that's not all Sagan brought. With his engaging manner,
he was a televangelist for naturalism, a philosophy he held with

religious fervor. And logically so, for whatever you take as the starting point of your worldview does function, in effect, as your religion.[1]

Take Sagan's trademark phrase, "The Cosmos is all that is or ever was or ever will be" (the opening line in *Cosmos*, his book based on the television series).[2] Here, Sagan is capitalizing on liturgical forms. Ever since the early church, Christians have sung the Gloria Patri: "Glory be to the Father, and to the Son, and to the Holy Ghost; As it was in the beginning, is now, and ever shall be, world without end." Sagan is clearly offering a substitute liturgy, a cadence to the cosmos. The sheer fact that he capitalizes the word *Cosmos*, just as religious believers capitalize the word *God*, is a dead giveaway that he is gripped by religious fervor.

In Sagan's television program and books, he makes it clear that he has no use for the transcendent Creator revealed in the Bible. The cosmos is his deity. In one of his many best-selling books, Sagan mockingly describes the Christian God as "an out-sized, light-skinned male with a long white beard, sitting on a throne somewhere up there in the sky, busily tallying the fall of every sparrow."[3] Sagan regards the cosmos as the only self-existing, eternal being: "A universe that is infinitely old requires no Creator."[4]

On point after point, Sagan offers a naturalistic substitute for traditional religion. While Christianity teaches that we are children of God, Sagan says that "we are, in the most profound sense, children of the Cosmos," for it is the cosmos that gave us birth and daily sustains us.[5] In a passage that is almost certainly auto-biographical, Sagan hints that the astronomer's urge to explore the cosmos is motivated by a mystical recognition that the chemicals in our bodies were originally forged in space—that outer space is our origin and our true home: "Some part of our being knows this is from where we came. We long to return."[6] And the astronomer's "awe" is nothing less than religious worship. "Our ancestors worshiped the Sun, and they were far from foolish." For if we must worship something, "does it not make sense to revere the Sun and the stars?"[7]

Like any religion, Sagan's worship of the cosmos prescribes certain moral duties for its adherents. The cosmos has created human life in its own image—"Our matter, our form, and much of our character is determined by the deep connection between life and the Cosmos"—and in return, we have a moral duty to the cosmos.[8] What is that duty? It is an "obligation to survive," an obligation we owe "to that Cosmos, ancient and vast, from which we spring."[9]

Salvation Themes

Sagan's worship of the cosmos even tells us how to be saved. Threats to human survival—pollution, war, food shortages— have nothing to do with moral failings. Instead, they result from technological incompetence, Sagan writes, which is hardly surprising since he believes that humanity is still in its evolutionary childhood.[10] As a result, the solutions may well come from more advanced civilizations somewhere out there, descending to Earth to save us. For this reason Sagan was an avid supporter of efforts to scan the far reaches of space for radio messages.[11] "The receipt of a single message from space would show that it is possible to live through such technological adolescence," he writes breathlessly, for it would prove that an advanced extraterrestrial race has survived the same stage and gone on to maturity.[12]

If this isn't a vision of salvation, what is? The cosmos will speak to us. It is there, and it is not silent.

In every human being is a deep, ongoing search for meaning and transcendence—part of the image of God in our very nature. Even if we flee God, the religious imprint remains. Everyone worships some kind of god. Everyone believes in some kind of deity—even if that deity is an impersonal substance such as matter, energy, or nature. That's why the Bible preaches against idolatry, not atheism. Naturalism may parade as science, marshaling facts and figures, but it is a religion.

PERVASIVE TEACHING

This religion is being taught everywhere in the public square today—even in the books your child reads in school or checks out of the public library. Not long ago, Nancy picked up a Berenstain Bears book for her young son. In the book, the Bear family invites the young reader to join them for a nature walk. We start out on a sunny morning, and after running into a few spiderwebs, we read in capital letters sprawled across a sunrise, glazed with light rays, those familiar words: Nature is "all that IS, or WAS, or EVER WILL BE!"[13]

Sound familiar? Of course. It is Sagan's famous opening line, now framed in cute images of little bears and bugs and birds—the philosophy of naturalism peddled for toddlers. And to drive the point home, the authors have drawn a bear pointing directly at the reader—your impressionable young child—and saying, "Nature is you! Nature is me!"[14] Human beings, too, are nothing more than parts of nature.

Is there any more poignant example of why Christians need to learn how to argue persuasively against naturalism? It is pressed on our children's imaginations long before they can think rationally and critically. It is presented everywhere as the only worldview supported by science. And it is diametrically opposed to Christianity.

The Christian must be ready to separate genuine science from philosophy. Evolution, as it is typically presented in textbooks and museums, confuses the two, presenting as "science" what is actually naturalistic philosophy. Indeed, many secular scientists insist that only naturalistic explanations qualify as science.

But why should we let secularists make the definitions? Let's be clear on the distinction between empirical science and philosophy, and then let's answer science with science and philosophy with philosophy.

BREAKING THE STEREOTYPE

This becomes all the more imperative when we realize what we're up against. The moment a Christian questions evolution, he or she is labeled a backwoods Bible-thumper, an ignorant reactionary who is trying to halt the progress of science. Like Katy, most schoolchildren today have seen the movie *Inherit the Wind* (or its counterpart on television), and their imaginations are peopled with blustery, ignorant Christians going toe-to-toe with intelligent, educated, urbane defenders of Darwin. When we question Darwinism in public, we are viewed through the grid portrayed in these media pieces.

Our first task, then, before we can even expect to be heard, is to shatter that grid, to break that stereotype. We must convince people that the debate is not about the Bible versus science. The debate is about pursuing an unbiased examination of the scientific facts and following those facts wherever they may lead. We must challenge the assumption that science by definition means naturalistic philosophy.

The real battle is worldview against worldview, religion against religion. On one side is the naturalistic worldview, claiming that the universe is the product of blind, purposeless forces. On the other side stands the Christian worldview, telling us we were created by a transcendent God who loves us and has a purpose for us. Nature itself is covered with his "fingerprints," marks of purpose in every area of scientific investigation. Our case is fully defensible, if only we learn how to make it.

THE STARTING POINT

The Christian worldview begins with the Creation, with a
deliberate act by a personal Being who existed from all eternity.
This personal dimension is crucial for understanding Creation.
Before bringing the world into existence, the Creator made a
choice, a decision: He set out a plan, an intelligent design.

According to the apostle Paul's writings, this design, which
gives the world its form and structure, is evident to all. "What
may be known about God is plain to them," Paul writes,
"because God has made it plain to them" (Rom. 1:19). How?
In the form and complexity of the world he made: "For since
the creation of the world God's invisible qualities—his eternal
power and divine nature—have been clearly seen, being understood from what has been made" (Rom. 1:20). Even unbelievers
know somewhere deep within that God must exist. Therefore,
"they are without excuse" (Rom. 1:20, NASB). In other words,
Paul teaches that those who look honestly at the world around
them should be able to conclude that it was created by an intelligent Being.

In the chapters that follow, we will look over Dave Mulholland's shoulder in his search for answers to his daughter's
questions. Was Sagan right, or was the apostle right in teaching
that the evidence for creation can be clearly seen by all? Did
the universe create itself? Did life arise from a sea of chemicals?
Can you get the intricate complexity of plants and animals without an intelligence to guide the process?

What we will discover may be as startling to you as it was to
Dave.

DISCUSSION QUESTIONS

CHAPTER 1

1 What do you want for your children and other young people you know?

2 In terms of your children, what do you worry about—in the near future and in the years to come?

3 Give examples of how Christianity and its symbols have become "artifacts," as Dave and Katy found at Epcot Center's Norway exhibit.

4 What do your children (or other people you know) "have against Christianity"?

5 Summarize "the story" presented to Dave and Katy at Epcot Center.

6 Why or how is giving one's life to Christ different from watching and accepting ideas presented in a movie like *Inherit the Wind*?

7 Read aloud 1 Peter 3:13-16 (in several versions, if possible). What does this passage say to Dave's predicament? How does it encourage you in this study?

CHAPTER 2

8 In what ways are you "foolishly overconfident" in your approach to your children or neighbors?

9 Why is it easy to be overconfident?

10 What impression do naturalistic scientists give about themselves and about Christianity?

11 Summarize answers to these questions for chapter 2, given at the beginning of the chapter:

a. What is the fundamental assumption of naturalism? What makes this a faith-based assumption?

b. In what ways did Carl Sagan's *Cosmos* attempt to provide a substitute for the Christian religion?

c. In talking to others, how can we break the stereotypes of Christians being ignorant?

d. What is the starting point of the Christian worldview?

ROLE PLAY

Role plays can be "no pressure" ways for participants to practice explaining the Christian worldview to skeptics. At the end of the role play, observers might give feedback. Remember a few ground rules. Any comments from listeners should be made (and received) as encouragement, not as personal criticism. "You might add this point . . ."; "You might approach the 'challenging' person as a friend, not an adversary"; "You might start with a more basic premise. . . . "

Choose one option, depending on the size of your group and the group dynamics.

1. In front of the whole group, ask two people to volunteer to act out a conversation between a skeptic and a Christian. The large group can give constructive feedback. If time allows, another pair can follow.

2. Have all participants pair off. The two people can take turns assuming the roles of a Christian and of a skeptic.

3. Have people make groups of three. One person takes the role of the Christian. The second person takes the role of a skeptic. The third is an observer who gives feedback. Alternate roles.

CONVERSATION STARTER

Assume a teenager or neighbor, like Katy, says to you, "Science is things that are proved," and insinuates that Christians need God just to make them feel good.

If this role play is difficult, don't give up. The information in the rest of the book will provide more information and rationale for the Christian worldview.

CLOSING SUMMARY

What is the most important point you want to remember from this session?

Consider sharing this with the group.

WAS THERE A BEGINNING?
IS THERE A DESIGN?

[Design] is the most empirical of the arguments for God [based on] observational premises about the kind of order we discover in nature.

FREDERICK FERRÉ

LET'S START AT THE VERY BEGINNING

As you read, keep the following questions in mind:
- What laws of thermodynamics undercut the eternal existence of the universe?
- How does naturalism regard reality? How does the big bang theory counter this view of reality?
- In what ways do scientists still disregard the evidence for a beginning point?
- What examples easily support the anthropic principle?
- In what unscientific ways do scientists explain the anthropic principle?

The first question any worldview must answer is how it all started. How did the universe begin? Dave Mulholland was about to discover one of the most exciting breakthroughs in recent scientific research, for in the past few decades, science has completely reversed itself on the question of the origin of the universe. After maintaining for centuries that the physical universe is eternal and therefore needs no creator, science today has uncovered dramatic new evidence that the universe did have an ultimate origin, that it began at a finite time in the past—just as the Bible teaches.

REVOLUTIONARY REVERSAL

To grasp just how revolutionary this is, we must understand that most ancient cultures believed that the universe is eternal—or, more precisely, that it was formed from some kind of primordial material that is eternal. The ancient Greeks even argued that the idea of an ultimate beginning was rationally inconceivable. Their arguments were revived during the late Middle Ages and Renaissance, when classical literature was rediscovered. Then, in the eighteenth century, scientists formulated the law of conservation of matter (that matter can be neither created nor destroyed), and it became a potent weapon in the hands of ardent materialists, who argued that science itself now ruled out any ultimate creation. "Today the indestructibility or permanence of matter is a scientific fact," wrote a nineteenth-century proponent of materialism. "Those who talk about an independent or supernatural creative force" that created the universe out of nothing "are in antagonism with the first and simplest axiom of a philosophical view of nature."[1]

And there things stood. The idea that the universe had a beginning was reduced to a bare article of religious faith, standing in lonely opposition to firmly established science.

Then, in the early twentieth century, several lines of evidence began a curious convergence: the implication from general relativity theory that the universe is expanding; the finding that the stars exhibit a "red shift," implying that they are moving outward; and finally, the realization that <u>the two laws of thermodynamics actually make it imperative to believe in a beginning to the universe.</u>

The second law of thermodynamics, the law of decay, implies that the universe is in a process of gradual disintegration—implacably moving toward final darkness and decay. In other words, the universe is running down, like a wound-up clock. And if it is running down, then there must have been a time when it was wound up. In the eloquent words of Lincoln Barnett in *The Universe and Dr. Einstein,* "the inescapable inference is that everything had a *beginning:* somehow and sometime the cosmic processes were started, the stellar fires ignited, and the whole vast pageant of the universe brought into being."[2]

What's more, the first law of thermodynamics (the conservation of matter) implies that matter cannot just pop into existence or create itself. And therefore, if the universe had a beginning, then something *external* to the universe must have caused it to come into existence—something, or Someone, transcendent to the natural world. As a result, the idea of creation is no longer merely a matter of religious faith; it is a conclusion based on the most straightforward reading of the scientific evidence. British physicist Paul Davies, though not a professing Christian, says the big bang is "the one place in the universe where there is room, even for the most hard-nosed materialist, to admit God."[3]

WAS THERE AN ULTIMATE BEGINNING?

These various lines of evidence coalesced in the 1960s and led to the formulation of big bang theory, which asserts that the universe began with a cosmic explosion. The new theory hit the scientific world like a thunderclap. It meant that the idea of an ultimate beginning was no longer merely religious dogma. Science itself now indicated that the universe burst into existence at a particular time in the remote past.

Big bang theory delivers a near fatal blow to naturalistic philosophy, for <u>the naturalistic credo regards reality as an unbroken sequence of cause and effect that can be traced back endlessly.</u> But the big bang represents a sudden discontinuity in the chain of cause and effect. It means science can trace events back in time only to a certain point; at the moment of the big bang explosion, science reaches an abrupt break, an absolute barrier. In fact, when

the theory was first proposed, a large number of scientists resisted
it for that very reason. The great physicist Arthur Eddington
summed up the feelings of many of his colleagues when he stated
that the idea of a beginning is philosophically "repugnant."[4]
Albert Einstein fiddled with his equations in the vain hope
of avoiding the conclusion that the universe had a beginning.
Astronomer Robert Jastrow, an agnostic who nevertheless
delights in tweaking the noses of his naturalistically minded colleagues, maintains that science has reached its limit, that it will
never be able to discover whether the agent of creation was "the
personal God of the Old Testament or one of the familiar forces
of physics."[5]

Ways Naturalists React to Ultimate Beginning

Squirm to Avoid Implications. Yet many secularists are still squirming to avoid the clear implications of the theory. Some argue that
the big bang actually advances naturalistic philosophy—that it
has extended naturalistic explanations back to the moment of the
origin of the universe itself. That means that if God exists, he has
been pushed back to a shadowy first cause who merely started
things off, with no role to play after that. But this is sheer bluster.
Far from supporting naturalism, big bang theory shows the *limits*
of all naturalistic accounts of reality by revealing that nature
itself—time, space, and matter—came into existence a finite
period of time ago.

Ignore Implications as "Religion." Perhaps the most common
strategy among scientists and educators today is simply to ignore
the startling implications of the big bang, labeling them "philosophy" or "religion" and shunting them aside. We deal only with
science, they say. Discussion of the ultimate cause *behind* the
big bang is dismissed as philosophy and is given no place in the
science classroom. As a result, schoolchildren never dream what
fascinating vistas are veiled from their sight, what interesting

questions they are essentially forbidden to ask. This is the approach Dave Mulholland witnessed at Disney World, when Bill-Nye-the-Science-Guy, with theatrical flourish, directed the audience's attention to an artistic rendering of the big bang. A thundering wave of light swept over the screen, but not a word was uttered about what came before the primeval explosion or what caused it.

Tweak the Theories. Still other scientists try to get around the big bang by tweaking the theory in ways that allow them to insist that matter is eternal after all. For example, Carl Sagan proposed that the explosion that started our universe was only one of a series—that the universe is expanding today, but at some point the process will reverse itself and begin to contract, until it is once again a tiny point, which will then explode once again, starting the entire process over. This oscillation will go on forever in endless repetition, like an accordion opening and closing.[6] But Sagan's speculation runs up against the basic laws of physics: Even an oscillating universe would use up the available energy in each cycle, and it would eventually run down. The second law of thermodynamics, the law of decay, shoots down any notion of an eternal universe.[7]

Craft Illogical Notions. Other scientists face the facts of an ultimate beginning, but in an effort to avoid the idea of a creator, they craft notions that are, frankly, illogical. Some speak of the self-generation of the universe, overlooking the obvious logical contradiction in such a notion (if the universe doesn't exist yet, there is no "self" to do the generating.) Others, like Stephen Hawking of Cambridge University, probably the best-known theoretical physicist today, propose that the early universe existed in "imaginary time," an idea that is for all purposes little more than fantasy. Still others have proposed that the universe simply popped into existence—completely uncaused—out of nothing. For example, philosophy professor Quentin Smith proposes that the universe "came from nothing, by nothing, for nothing."[8] But this is to leave the domain of science for sheer magic. One of the most established laws of experience is that something cannot come out of nothing.

Naturalists simply have no way to avoid the challenge posed by the big bang without twisting themselves into impossible logical contortions. The facts clearly indicate that the universe is not eternal, and it cannot originate itself. The implication is that the universe began at a definite moment in time, in a flash of light and energy. Science has begun to sound eerily like Genesis 1: "And God said, 'Let there be light' " (1:3).

Breaking the Stereotype

These are arguments we can make when we encounter people hostile to Christian faith. One day my wife, Patty, came home from a Bible study and told me how outraged the entire group was over an episode at the local school. One of the women in the group had a thirteen-year-old son who had received a low grade for giving a wrong answer on his weekly quiz for his earth science class. To the question "Where did Earth come from?" Tim had written, "God created it." His test came back with a big red check and twenty points marked off his grade. The "correct" answer, according to the teacher, was that Earth is the product of the big bang.

The women in Patty's Bible study urged Tim's mother to march into the classroom and show the teacher what the Bible says. "It's right there in Genesis 1," they said. "*God* created the heavens and the earth."

But as soon as Patty told me the story, I reached for the phone to call Tim's mother. "Don't go to the teacher with Bible in hand," I said.

She was taken aback. "But the Bible shows that the teacher was wrong."

"As believers, we know that Scripture is inspired and authoritative," I explained, "but Tim's teacher will dismiss it out of hand. She'll say, 'That's religion. I teach science.' "

What we need to avoid in such situations is giving the mistaken idea that Christianity is opposed to science. If we are too quick to quote the Bible, we will never break out of the stereotype spread by *Inherit the Wind*. We should not oppose science with religion; we should oppose *bad* science with *better* science.

We ought to raise questions such as What came before the big bang? What caused it? If the big bang was the origin of the universe itself, then its cause must be something *outside* the universe. The truth is that big bang theory gives dramatic support to the biblical teaching that the universe had an ultimate beginning— that space, matter, and time itself are finite. Far from being a challenge to Christian faith, as Tim's teacher seemed to think, the theory actually gives startling evidence *for* the faith.

And the case for creation is even stronger if we look at the *nature* of our universe. It is a universe that speaks at every turn of design and purpose.

WAS IT ALL A COINCIDENCE?

In the days and weeks after coming home from his vacation with Katy at Disney World, Dave Mulholland could hear the phrases from various exhibits reverberating over and over again in his memory, like a CD on replay, each time hammering in a sense of helplessness as he realized he had no good answers. He mimicked the message from "The Living Seas" with grim irony: A small sphere, the planet Earth, "just happened" to be the right size and "just happened" to be the right distance from the sun so that life "just happened" to arise. And through a process of random mutations and natural selection, we humans "just happened" to appear on the scene.

What a message for kids to hear, Dave groaned. *It tells them they're nothing more than a cosmic accident. Small wonder that, over time, language about a loving God who created them and loves them sounds more and more like a fairy tale.*

But are all these coincidences really just . . . coincidences? Or did Someone design the universe this way? This was the second question Dave was determined to tackle. He set about studying just as he had in college—by collecting books and articles on the subject. And what he discovered, to his surprise, is another dramatic shift in recent scientific thought. Not only are scientists acknowledging an ultimate beginning, but they are also recognizing that the physical structure of the universe gives striking evidence of purpose and design. They have proposed what is known as <u>the *anthropic principle,* which states that the physical structure of the universe is exactly what it must be in order to support life.</u>

The Anthropic Principle

After the first spacecraft landed on the moon, one stunning photograph quickly became familiar to all Americans: a view of the cloud-wrapped Earth, seen just above the horizon of the black and cratered surface of the moon. The contrast was striking. Our beautiful blue-and-white planet, so hospitable to life, seen against the stark, barren, lifeless lunar landscape.

Yet even the moon is a friendly place compared to Venus, where a rain of sulfuric acid falls toward a surface as hot as boiling lead. And even Venus is hospitable compared to the icy crystals that make up Jupiter, with frozen clouds of gas stretching across its surface, giving the planet its striped look. And even Jupiter might be considered approachable compared to the million-degree temperature inside the stars or compared to the immense reaches of hard vacuum between them.

From the perspective of the space age, it has become clearer than ever that Earth is unique. It boasts a wealth of characteristics that make it capable of supporting life—a nearly endless list of preconditions that have been exquisitely met only, as far as we know, on our planet.

How does Earth happen to be so special? Is it just coincidence? Luck? Or was it designed by a loving Creator who had us in mind from the outset?

Earth's Orbit

Consider, for example, Earth's orbit. "The Living Seas" exhibit is quite right in describing Earth as "a small sphere of just the right size [that] lies just the right distance from its mother star." If Earth were even slightly closer to the sun, all its water would boil away, and life would be impossible. On the other hand, if Earth were only slightly farther away from the sun, all its water would freeze, and the terrestrial landscape would be nothing but barren deserts.

And it's not only the landscape that is affected by the position of our planet. The processes inside our bodies also rely on these hospitable conditions. The chemical reactions necessary for life to function occur within a narrow temperature range, and Earth is exactly the right distance from the sun to fall within that range. What's more, for all this to happen, Earth must remain about the same distance from the sun in its orbit; that is, its orbit must be nearly circular—which it is, in contrast to the elliptical orbits of most other planets in our solar system.

Are these finely calibrated distances a product of mere happenstance? Or were they *designed* to support life?

The Wonder of Water

For another example, consider the existence of water, that common substance we take for granted. Water has a host of unique properties absolutely indispensable for life. For example, it is the only known substance whose solid phase (ice) is less dense than its liquid phase. This is why ice forms on the top of oceans and lakes instead of on the bottom, allowing fish and other marine life to survive the winter. On the microscopic level, water molecules exhibit something called the hydrophobic effect, which gives water the unique ability to shape proteins and nucleic acids in DNA. From a molecular standpoint, "the various properties of water are nothing short of miraculous," writes Michael Corey in *God and the New Cosmology;* "no other compound even comes close to duplicating its many life-supporting properties."[9]

Cosmic Qualities

But Earth could not support life unless the cosmos itself had the right physical properties. The anthropic principle draws together a staggering number of "cosmic coincidences" that make life possible. For example, the big bang had to have exploded with just the right degree of vigor for our present universe to have formed. If it had occurred with too *little* velocity, the universe would have collapsed back in on itself shortly after the big bang because of gravitational forces; if it had occurred with too *much* velocity, the matter would have streaked away so fast that it would have been impossible for galaxies and solar systems to subsequently form. To state it another way, the force of gravity must be fine-tuned to allow the universe to expand at precisely the right rate (accurate to within 1 part in 10^{60}). The fact that the force of gravity just happens to be the right number with "such stunning accuracy," writes physicist Paul Davies, "is surely one of the great mysteries of cosmology."[10]

Atomic Structure and Balance

Take another example: the structure of the atom. Everything in the universe is made of atoms, from the stars in the farthest heavens to the cells in the human body—and the atom itself is a bundle of fortuitous "coincidences." Within the atom, the neutron is just slightly more massive than the proton, which means that free neutrons (those not trapped within an atom) can decay and turn into protons. If things were reversed—if it were the proton that was larger and had a tendency to decay—the very structure of the universe would be impossible.

Why? Because a free proton is simply a hydrogen atom, and if free protons had a tendency to decay, then everything made of hydrogen would decay. The sun, which is made of hydrogen, would melt away. Water, a liquid oxide of hydrogen (H_2O) would be impossible. In fact, the universe itself would decay, since about 74 percent of the observed universe consists of hydrogen.

And why is the neutron larger than the proton? No one knows. There is no physical cause to explain why the neutron is larger. It is simply a fact. So apparently the only "reason" for the difference in size is that it allows the universe to exist and to support life.

Not only do atomic particles have a size, but they also have an electrical charge. What child hasn't delighted in rubbing his feet on the carpet and giving people a shock by touching them? This annoying practice works because rubbing the carpet knocks off some of the electrons and gives the child a negative charge.

Within the atom, electrons have a negative charge, and protons have a positive charge. Yet, aside from carpet-rubbing pranksters or socks that stick together in the dryer, most of the objects we encounter in daily life have no electrical charge. Why not? Because the charge of the proton exactly balances that of the electron.

And it's a good thing it does. If the electron carried more charge than the proton, all atoms would be negatively charged. In that case—since identical charges repel—all the atoms composing all the objects in the universe would fly apart in a catastrophic explosion. On the other hand, if the proton carried more charge than the electron, all atoms would be positively charged—with the same disastrous consequences.

There is no known physical reason, no natural explanation, for the precise balance in the electrical charges of the proton and the electron—especially when you consider that the two particles differ from one another in all other respects: in size, weight, magnetic properties, and so on. And since there is no natural explanation, no natural law to account for this extraordinarily precise adjustment, is it not reasonable to conclude that this intricate arrangement is the product of a choice, a plan, a design?

And More

The list of "coincidences" goes on and on. It turns out that the slightest tinkering with the values of the fundamental forces of physics—gravity, electromagnetism, the strong and weak nuclear forces—would have resulted in a universe where life was utterly impossible. The anthropic principle states that in our own universe, all these seemingly arbitrary and unrelated values in physics have one strange thing in common: They are precisely the values needed to get a universe capable of supporting life.

The term *anthropic principle* comes from the Greek word *anthropos*, which means human being, and it begins to appear that the laws of physics were exquisitely calibrated from the outset for the creation of human life. Of course, many scientists shy away from this conclusion because it presupposes a creator, and they have been trained to believe that such a concept has no place in science. So what do they do about these obvious marks of design and purpose in the universe? They scramble to explain them away, searching for ways to account for design in the universe without having to acknowledge a designer. Yet, ironically, all these attempts to explain away the design turn out to be far *less* scientific than a straightforward acknowledgment of a creator.

WAYS NATURALISTS REACT TO THE ANTHROPIC PRINCIPLE

The "Many Worlds" Hypothesis. One of the widely held versions of the anthropic principle is the "many worlds" hypothesis. According to this theory, an infinite number of universes exist, all with different laws and different values for fundamental numbers. Most of these universes are dark, lifeless places. But by sheer probability, some will have just the right structure to support life. The "fit" universes survive, while the "unfit" are weeded out. Our own, of course, happens to be a universe "fit" for life.

But how do we know whether these numberless other universes really exist? The answer is, we *cannot* know. The idea is purely a product of scientific imagination. Even if alternative universes did exist, they would be inherently impossible for science to detect. Candid scientists admit that the whole idea is motivated by a desire to avoid the theological implications of the anthropic principle. Physicist Heinz Pagels says that if the universe appears to be tailor-made for life, the most straightforward conclusion is that it *was* tailor-made, created by a transcendent God; it is only because many scientists find that conclusion "unattractive" that they adopt the theory of multiple universes, Pagels explains. And he adds wryly, "It is the closest that some atheists can get to God." In other words, atheists are squirming every which way to avoid the obvious.[11]

The Universe as Quasi-Intelligent Being

Another version is the *participatory anthropic principle.* Drawing a wild extrapolation from quantum mechanics, this version says that the universe did not fully exist until human beings emerged to observe it. And so, in order to become fully real, the universe decided to evolve human consciousness. In the words of Nobel prize–winning biologist George Wald, "The universe wants to be known."[12]

This is indeed a strange picture of the universe—as if it had
a heart, longing to be known, and a mind, deciding to evolve
human beings. Yet it seems to be a picture shared by physicist
Freeman Dyson, who says, "I find that the universe in some
sense must have known that we were coming."[13] And astronomer George Greenstein echoes a similar refrain: "If this is the
best way to make a universe, how did the universe find that
out?"[14]

Here we have a concept of the universe as a quasi-intelligent
being that can know and be known, that can plot and plan. It
is astonishing that scientists will dismiss the idea of a Creator
as unscientific, yet turn around and embrace the bizarre, almost
mystical concept of a conscious universe.

Motives?

Scientists are not being forced to these speculative forms of the
anthropic principle by the facts; instead, they are driven by a
religious motive—or rather, by an *anti*religious motive. So
strong is their desire to avoid the conclusion of divine creation
that they will resort to irrational notions, such as the existence
of millions of unknowable universes or a pantheistic universe
that "knew" we were coming. In the words of Patrick Glynn of
George Washington University, the fact that so many scientists
are willing to accept "wild speculations about unseen universes
for which not a shred of observational evidence exists suggests
something about both the power of the modern atheistic ideology and the cultural agenda of many in the scientific profession."
Then Glynn delivers this searing indictment: "The mainstream
scientific community has in effect shown its attachment to the
atheistic ideology of the random universe to be in some respects
more powerful than its commitment to the scientific method
itself."[15]

Precisely.

The Marks of Design

The anthropic principle acknowledges that we can identify and recognize the products of design, and that many of the features of the physical universe bear the marks of design. In many ways, the scientific method is merely the codification of common sense, and the detection of design is no exception. I remember as a child visiting the "Old Man in the Mountains," a tourist attraction in New Hampshire's White Mountains. At an overlook station, our family would join other eager tourists to see if we could detect, in the outline of the rocks, what looked like the profile of an old man. Of course, we knew it wasn't really a carving of a man; it was like many other places that are billed as natural wonders—places where, over the ages, the wind and rain have carved out shapes that resemble a face or a bridge or some other familiar object.

By contrast, imagine you are driving through South Dakota and suddenly come upon a mountain bearing the unmistakable likenesses of four American presidents, looking just as you remember them from your history books. Instantly you recognize Lincoln's jutting chin and Washington's high forehead. Would you—would anyone?—conclude that these shapes were the product of wind or rain or glacial erosion? Of course not. Immediately you realize that artists with chisels and drills have painstakingly carved these four famous faces out of the stone.

We intuitively recognize the products of design versus the products of natural forces. And in his exciting new book *The Design Inference,* mathematician William Dembski has offered an "explanatory filter" to give logical form to this intuition. When we try to explain any natural phenomenon, there are three possibilities: chance, law, or design. If the natural phenomenon is irregular, erratic, and unspecified, we conclude that it is a random event. If it is regular, repeatable, and predictable, we conclude that it is the result of natural forces. But if it is unpredictable and yet highly specified, we conclude that it is designed. The four presidents' faces on Mt. Rushmore are irregular (not something we see happening generally as the result of erosion), yet specified (they fit a particular, preselected pattern). Applying the explanatory filter, the evidence clearly points to design.[16]

According to the anthropic principle, evidence for design is found throughout the physical universe. If we apply Dembski's explanatory filter, we find that many of the major features of the physical universe are irregular (there is no natural law accounting for them) and highly specified (they appear preselected to support life). In short, they bear the unmistakable characteristics of design.

And if the universe exhibits design, it is logical to conclude that there is a designer. The most obvious inference is that the universe *appears* to be designed because it *is* designed—powerful evidence for the biblical worldview that a loving God created the world.

That answers the question about the ultimate origin of the universe. But what happened after that? Where did living things come from? Did life evolve from the merging of molecules in a primordial sea?

Dave knew his search for answers had only begun.

*A little science estranges a man
from God. A lot of science brings
him back.*   FRANCIS BACON

LIFE IN A TEST TUBE?

As you read, keep the following questions in mind:

- What properties of amino acids and functional proteins make their chance development implausible?
- When scientists try to duplicate what "might have happened," in what ways do they rig the experiments?
- If the discovery of DNA discounts a "chance" theory of origins, what have naturalists put in the place of "chance"?
- How does the discovery of DNA support the idea of design and creation?
- How does the high information content of DNA bolster the argument for design?

You don't have to drive to Disney World to indoctrinate your kids in the Gospel according to Evolution. Whose toddler these days doesn't know *The Land Before Time* video series? There's no debating that the little dinosaurs are endearing, but along with the story, each video offers an excursion into evolution. Children sit wide-eyed, watching primal one-celled organisms arise out of the blue-green churning seas—organisms that "change again and again," until they finally evolve into cute little dinos.[1] It is a delightful, fairy-tale introduction to naturalistic evolution. And once a child's imagination is populated with these bright images, it is nearly impossible for a parent to dislodge them. When the imagination is later bolstered with classroom teaching, Christian parents like Dave face an uphill battle.

So let's peel back the colorful images to look for the cold, sober truth about the origin of life. Have scientists created life in a test tube? Have they proven that life arose from a primordial soup?

MILLER'S MIX

The way scientists try to prove that life arose in the primitive seas is to re-create the same conditions in the laboratory and see what happens. One of the best-known experiments occurred in 1953. Newspapers across the country carried photos of Stanley Miller of the University of Chicago, wearing a white laboratory coat and heavy square-rimmed glasses, reporting his sensational claim that he had accomplished the first step toward creating life in a test tube.

Miller had mixed simple chemicals and gases in a glass tube, then zapped them with an electrical charge to induce chemical reactions. The idea was to simulate conditions on the early earth and show that simple chemicals could indeed have reacted to create the building blocks of life. To everyone's surprise, what emerged at the other end of the laboratory apparatus were amino acids, the building blocks of protein, an important constituent of living things. The news was electrifying. Few people had dared dream that the elements of a living cell could be produced under conditions allegedly existing on the early earth. Miller's success seemed to provide dramatic evidence for a naturalistic account of life's origin.

It also set off a domino series of similar experiments, some using heat as an energy source instead of Miller's electrical charge, others using ultraviolet light to simulate light from the sun. Most of these experiments have succeeded in producing amino acids, and the amino acids have even linked up in chains resembling proteins. The results have been reported in one breathless headline after another.

The problem with all this frenetic activity is that no one is asking critical questions about what the experiments really prove. The conventional wisdom is that they support the theory that life evolved spontaneously from simple chemicals in a primeval pond about four billion years ago. But do they?[2]

Fifty-Fifty Amino Mix

Let's start with the amino acids that came out of Miller's test tube. The truth is that these differ in critical ways from those found in living things. Amino acids come in two forms, what scientists call left-handed and right-handed. Living things are highly selective: They use only the left-handed form. But when Miller and his colleagues mixed chemicals in the laboratory, they got both kinds— an even fifty-fifty mix of left-handed and right-handed. In fact, this is what happens every time anyone mixes the chemicals randomly in the laboratory. There is no natural process that produces only left-handed amino acids, the kind required by living things. All of this means that the amino acids formed in the test tube are useless for life.

Link and Sequence?

And that's only the first problem. The next step to "creating life" is to get amino acids to link up and form proteins. In 1958 Sidney Fox, a chemist at the University of Miami, started with already existing amino acids and boiled them in water to induce them to react with one another. The result was proteinlike chains of amino acids, and, like Miller, Fox was promptly inducted into the Modern Hall of Scientific Heroes.

But serious problems are hidden beneath the hype, because once again, life is much more selective than anything we get from a test tube. The proteins in living things are comprised of amino acids hooked together in a very particular chemical bond called a peptide bond. But amino acids are like Tinkertoy pieces: They're capable of hooking together in all sorts of different ways, forming several different chemical bonds. And in the test tube, that's exactly what they do. They hook up in a variety of ways, never producing a genuine protein capable of functioning in a living cell.

In addition, for a protein to be functional, the amino acids must link up in a particular sequence, just like the sequence of letters in a sentence. If you scramble the letters in a sentence, you get nonsense; if you scramble the amino acids in a protein, you get a nonfunctional protein. Yet in laboratory experiments, all we get are scrambled, random sequences. There's no natural force capable of selecting the right amino acids and lining them up in the right order. As a result, the proteinlike chains that appear in the test tube are useless for life.

The fact is, the much-touted experiments tell us very little about where real, functional proteins came from. Yet this inconvenient fact is rarely mentioned when headlines blare out the news that scientists have succeeded in creating the building blocks of life.

WAYS SCIENTISTS "CHEAT"

And there's more. If scientists really wanted to duplicate what might have happened in a primordial soup billions of years ago, they would simply mix up some chemicals in a vat, expose them to an energy source (heat or light), and see what happens. Yet no one ever does this. Why not? Because it is impossible to get any important chemical compounds that way. Instead, to get even useless, nonfunctional amino acids and proteins, researchers have to control the experiment in various ways.

Pure and Fresh Ingredients

For example, in nature, chemicals are almost never found in a pure state. As a result, one cannot predict with confidence which reactions will take place. Substances A and B might react effectively in the laboratory, where isolated and purified forms are used. But out in nature, there are almost always other chemicals— C and D—lying about, which means substance A might react with C instead of with B, yielding a completely different result from what the scientist expected. In other words, out in nature there are all kinds of competing reactions.

So how do scientists avoid the problem of competing reactions? They uncap their bottles and pour out only pure isolated ingredients. And when the experiment involves more than one step, such as going from amino acids to proteins, researchers start over each step with fresh ingredients. Obviously, this rigs the experiment. Nature doesn't have flasks of pure ingredients to pour out at each step of the way.

Screening Ultraviolet Light

Or consider another typical experiment, one that uses ultraviolet light instead of electricity to get the chemicals to react. The idea is to simulate sunlight beaming down on a primeval pond on the early earth. There's just one little problem: The longer wavelengths of ultraviolet light are very destructive and would destroy the very amino acids that scientists are hoping to get. So what do they do? They screen out the longer wavelengths and use only shorter wavelengths.

But once again, success is bought at the price of rigging the experiment. A real primeval pond would have no screens to protect the fragile amino acids from destructive wavelengths of sunlight. As a result, these experiments don't tell us what could realistically have happened on the early earth; they tell us only what happens when researchers carefully control the conditions.

Protective Traps

Another device that every origin-of-life experiment resorts to is the use of a trap to protect the end products after they have formed. Amino acids are delicate, and they easily break down into the elements of which they are composed. When electricity or heat is used as an energy source to induce the chemicals to link up and form amino acids, that same energy can also break them back down. Hence the researcher has to find some way to protect the delicate chemical compounds.

The solution is to build a trap that removes the amino acids from the reaction site as soon as they form, to protect them from disintegrating. Miller's apparatus was a square of glass tubing with a bulb on top, bristling with electrodes to create sparks, and a U-shaped bulge on the bottom, filled with water to trap the amino acids. Miller would drain the trap to remove the amino acids from the reaction area so they would not break down again.

To understand why this is so important, imagine you are a child eating a bowl of alphabet soup. When you stir the soup, you are an energy source. Stirring slowly, you might cause a few letters to line up and form short words, such as "T-O" or "A-N-D." But as you keep stirring, your spoon will quickly cause the letters to scatter again—unless you scoop the words out with your spoon and put them carefully on your plate. That's what the trap does: It takes amino acids out of harm's way and preserves them.

The trouble is that, once again, nature doesn't come equipped with handy traps to protect the delicate building blocks of life. Any amino acids that might form spontaneously in nature would disintegrate just as quickly. A trap is absolutely necessary for a successful experiment, but it just as surely makes the experiment completely irrelevant to confirming any naturalistic theory of life's origin.

The Message?

At every turn, the experiments that have ignited so much excitement turn out to be artificial. As a result, even the most successful origin-of-life experiments tell us next to nothing about what could have happened under natural conditions. They tell us only what happens when a brilliant scientist manipulates the conditions, "coaxing" the materials down the chemical pathways necessary to produce the building blocks of life.

So what do these experiments really prove? That *life can be created only by an intelligent agent directing, controlling, and manipulating the process.* The latest scientific findings do not discredit biblical faith; rather, they provide positive evidence that the origin of life requires an intelligent agent, a creator.

NOT A CHANCE

If we need additional confirmation, it comes from a surprising place: from the use of computers in biology. Long before the information age, the living cell was thought to be quite simple, and it was easy enough to think life arose by chance. Darwin himself thought the cell was a simple blob of protoplasm, and he conjectured that it evolved in a "warm little pond." But as science began uncovering the marvelous complexity of the cell, it became harder and harder to hold on to chance theories.

Biologists typically took refuge in the idea of nearly endless time. Given enough time, they argued, anything can happen. Over millions of years, the unlikely becomes likely, the improbable is transformed into the inevitable. And for a while, biologists got away with this argument—only because the number of millennia invoked were so immense that no one was capable of conceptualizing what that kind of time scale really meant.

Simulation Says "No Way"

But the computer revolution put an end to any chance theory of life's origin. Beginning in the 1960s, mathematicians began writing computer programs to simulate every process under the sun, and they cast their calculating eyes on evolution itself. Hunched over their high-speed computers, they simulated the trial-and-error processes of neo-Darwinian evolution over the equivalent of billions of years. The outcome was jolting: The computers showed that the probability of evolution by chance processes is essentially zero, no matter how long the time scale.[3]

In 1966, at a landmark symposium at the Wistar Institute in Philadelphia, a group of computer specialists presented their findings to the nation's biologists. The charge was led by Murray Eden of MIT and Marcel Schutzenberger of the University of Paris. At first, the biologists were angry at the upstart computer whizzes for invading their territory. But the numbers could not be denied. And after the symposium, chance theories began to be quietly buried.

As a result, today it is common to hear prominent scientists scoff at the idea that life arose by chance. The famous astronomer Sir Fred Hoyle compares it to lining up 10^{50} (ten with fifty zeros after it) blind people, giving each one a scrambled Rubik's Cube, and finding that they all solve the cube at the same moment.[4]

Neither Random Processes nor Compulsion of Forces

What has been put in the place of chance? For the naturalist who assumes life evolved spontaneously, there is only one other logical possibility: If life did not arise by random processes, then it must have arisen under the compulsion of forces in matter itself. Hence biologists working in the field today are searching for some force within matter that directed the process—some impulse that caused life to emerge. The assumption is that life will arise inevitably whenever conditions are right. A widely used college textbook sums up the approach in its title: *Biochemical Predestination.*[5]

Yet there is no agreement on *which* forces in matter are up to the job. Dean Kenyon of San Francisco State University, one of the original exponents of this doctrine and coauthor of *Biochemical*

Predestination, has since repudiated his own theory. If you look at the experiments, Kenyon explained in an interview, "one thing that stands out is that you do not get ordered sequences of amino acids. . . . If we thought we were going to see a lot of spontaneous ordering, something must have been wrong with our theory."[6] Kenyon has since accepted the idea of an intelligent Designer as the answer to the origin of life.

Support for Intelligent Design

Sadly, too few scientists have this kind of courage. Yet it is becoming ever clearer that the experiments fail to support any naturalistic theory of life's origin. What they *do* support is the idea of intelligent design. The experiments give positive evidence that life arises only when the raw materials are carefully selected, arranged, controlled, and organized by an intelligent cause.

The advance of science is not casting up new challenges to Christian faith, as we are so often told. Instead, it is uncovering ever more powerful evidence that what Christians believe is true on all levels, including the natural world. And that is becoming even clearer today as scientists learn more about what is inside the cell—and especially the structure of DNA.

DNA: THE LANGUAGE OF LIFE

We've all heard the term *DNA,* thanks to its use in controversial court cases like the O. J. Simpson trial, but few of us really understand what it is. Simply put, DNA is like a language in the heart of the cell, a molecular message, a set of instructions telling the cell how to construct proteins—much like the software needed to run a computer. Moreover, the amount of information DNA includes is staggering: A single cell of the human body contains as much information as the *Encyclopedia Britannica*—all thirty volumes—three or four times over. As a result, the question of the origin of life must now be redefined as the question of the origin of biological information. Can information arise by natural forces alone? Or does it require an intelligent agent?

Scientists committed to naturalism must try to construct an explanation of life based solely on physical-chemical laws. They must explain the information in DNA as a product of natural processes at work in the chemicals that comprise living things. Recall Katy's words to her father at Epcot: "It's chemicals. It's all chemicals."

Sequence by Natural Law or by Design?

It's true that DNA is composed of ordinary chemicals (bases, sugars, phosphates) that react according to ordinary laws. But what makes DNA function as a message is not the chemicals themselves but rather their *sequence,* their pattern. The chemicals in DNA are grouped into molecules (called nucleotides) that act like letters in a message, and they must be in a particular order if the message is going to be intelligible. If the letters are scrambled, the result is nonsense. So the crucial question comes down to whether the sequence of chemical "letters" arose by natural causes or whether it required an intelligent source. Is it the product of law or design?

EXAMPLES OF INTELLIGENT DESIGN

More than two hundred years ago, the English clergyman William Paley framed the classic argument for design by comparing a living organism to a watch. Upon finding a watch lying on the beach, no one would say, "Oh, look what the wind and the waves have produced." Instead, we instantly recognize that a watch has a structure that can be produced only by an intelligent agent. Likewise, Paley argued, living things have a type of structure that can be produced only by an intelligent cause.[7]

The naturalistic scientist insists that the idea of an intelligent cause has no place in science. But the truth is that several branches of science already use the concept of intelligence and have even devised tests for detecting the work of an intelligent agent. Consider forensic science. When police find a body, their first question is, Was this death the result of natural causes or foul play (an intentional act by an intelligent being)? Pathologists perform a battery of fairly straightforward tests to get an answer.

Likewise, when archeologists uncover an unusually shaped rock, they ask whether the shape is a result of weathering or whether the rock is a primitive tool, deliberately chipped by some ancient hunter. Again, certain tests are used to detect whether it is a product of intelligent activity.

When cryptographers are given a page of scrambled letters, how do they determine whether it is just a random sequence or a secret code? When radio signals are detected in outer space, how do astronomers know whether it is a message from another civilization? There are rules that can be applied to determine whether the letters or the signals fit the structure of a language.

For example, in 1967 astronomers were startled to discover radio pulses coming from outer space. "Our first thought," they said, was that "this was another intelligent race" trying to communicate with us, and they labeled the signals "LGM" (Little Green Men). However, further analysis showed that the pulses formed the wrong kind of pattern for a language. Instead of a new life-form, what they had discovered was a pulsar, a rotating star that mimics a radio beacon.[8]

In everyday life, we weigh natural versus intelligent causes all the time without thinking much about it. If we see ripples on a sandy beach, we assume they were formed by natural processes. But if we see words written in the sand—"John loves Mary"— immediately we recognize a different kind of order, and we know that a couple of lovers recently lingered there. Or consider the children's game of finding shapes in the clouds. As adults, we know the shapes are just the result of wind and temperature acting on the water molecules. But what if we see "clouds" that spell out a message? In the film *Reunion in France,* set in Nazi-occupied Paris in the 1940s, a plucky pilot flies over the city every day and uses skywriting to spell out the single word "COURAGE."[9] Had you and I been there, we would never have mistaken the sky-writing for an ordinary cloud; even though the words were white and fluffy, we would have been certain that natural forces did not create the message.

DNA, BETTER THAN A WATCH

In the same way, when scientists probed the nucleus of the cell, they came across something analogous to "John loves Mary" or "COUR-AGE"—the only difference being that DNA contains vastly more information. What this means is that we can now revive the design argument using a much closer analogy than Paley's analogy between living things and watches. The new analogy is between DNA and written messages. Are there natural forces capable of writing a book or programming a computer disk or writing a symphony? Clearly not. <u>The discovery of DNA provides powerful new evidence that life is the product of intelligent design.</u> It's an argument that is simple, easy to explain, and based solidly on experience.

High Information Content: By Nature or Design?

Since DNA contains information, the case can be stated even more strongly in terms of *information theory,* a field of research that investigates the ways information is transmitted. As we said earlier, the naturalistic scientist has only two possible ways to explain the origin of life—either chance or natural law. But information theory gives us a powerful tool for discounting both these explanations, for both chance and law lead to structures with low information content, whereas DNA has a very high information content.[10]

MINIMUM NUMBER OF INSTRUCTIONS

A structure or message is said to have high or low information content depending on the minimum number of instructions needed to tell you how to construct it. To illustrate, a random sequence of letters has low information content because it requires only two instructions: (1) select a letter of the English alphabet and write it down, and (2) do it again (select another letter and write it down). By the same token, a regular, repetitive pattern of letters has low information content as well. Using your computer to create Christmas wrapping paper requires only a few instructions: (1) type in "M-e-r-r-y C-h-r-i-s-t-m-a-s," and (2) do it again. By contrast, if you want your computer to print out the poem "The Night before Christmas," you must specify every letter, one by one. Because the process of writing down the poem requires a large number of instructions, it is said to have high information content.

Similarly, in nature, both random patterns and regular patterns (like ripples on a beach) have low information content. By contrast, DNA has a very high information content. It would be impossible to produce a simple set of instructions telling a chemist how to synthesize the DNA of even the simplest bacterium. You would have to specify every chemical "letter," one by one—and there are literally millions. So <u>DNA has a completely different structure from the products of either chance or natural law,</u> and information theory gives us the conceptual tools to debunk any such attempts to explain the origin of life.

ALL IN THE CRYSTALS?

As we noted earlier, most scientists today are looking for some kind of self-organizing force in matter itself to explain life's origin, and yet there are currently no real candidates. As a result, most treatments of the subject resort to analogies, pointing to

spontaneous ordering in *non*living structures, such as crystals.
Browse through the library, and you'll find many books that use
the analogy of crystal formation to explain how life might have
started.

But does this analogy work? Not at all, and information theory
cuts through the fog surrounding this subject. Whether they are
ordinary (like salt and sugar) or exquisite (like rubies and dia-
monds), all crystals are examples of repetitive order. The unique
structure of any crystal is the result of what we might think of as
the "shape" of its atoms (or ions), which causes them to slot into
a particular position and to layer themselves in a fixed, orderly
pattern. In salt, the atoms always form a six-sided box, whereas
sugar atoms always come together in a rectangular crystal slanted
on both ends. "If we could shrink ourselves to the atomic scale,"
writes zoologist Richard Dawkins in *The Blind Watchmaker,* "we
would see almost endless rows of atoms stretching to the horizon
in straight lines—galleries of geometric repetition."[11]

This "geometric repetition" is precisely the problem, for it
means crystals carry very little information. It's as if someone said,
"pick a shape" and "do it again." If the DNA molecule were really
analogous to a crystal, it would consist of a single pattern repeat-
ing again and again, like Christmas wrapping paper, so crystal
formation gives us no clue whatsoever to the origin of DNA.

Another attempt to find a naturalistic answer to the origin of
life comes from the new field of *complexity theory.* On their computer screens, researchers "grow" marvelous shapes that resemble
ferns and forests and snowflakes. This is being touted as the
answer to the spontaneous origin of order.

Is this new field of research finally going to uncover a law that
can account for the spontaneous origin of life itself? The verdict
is already in, and it is no. The truth is that the ferns and swirls
constructed by complexity theorists on their computer screens represent the same kind of order as crystals. In the words of Stuart

Kauffman of the Santa Fe Institute, the patterns are constructed by the repeated application of only a few "astonishingly simple rules."[12] In other words, like crystals, these structures can be specified with just a few instructions, followed by "do it again."[13]

CONCLUSION

The conclusion is that there are no known physical laws capable of creating a structure like DNA with high information content. Based on both the latest scientific knowledge and on ordinary experience, we know only one cause that is up to the task: an intelligent agent. Only an intelligent person can type out "The Night before Christmas" or devise a computer program or compose a musical score. And only an intelligent cause could create the information contained in the DNA molecule.

WHO'S RATIONAL?

Many Christians are nervous about invoking God to answer any scientific question, even the origin of life. We're afraid of being accused of resorting to the "God of the gaps" argument—of using God to cover over our ignorance—only to have a natural explanation turn up later and embarrass us. This fear is understandable, given the fact that Christians often have been cast into the same category as primitives who attribute thunder to the raging of their gods. But there are times when Christians ought to turn the tables on the critics. There are times when it is more rational to accept a supernatural explanation and when it is actually irrational to hold out for a natural explanation.

We know from science itself that there are some things nature cannot do. We know that we will never fulfill the alchemists' dream of chemically transmuting lead into gold. We know that a parent of one species will never give birth to offspring of another species. To persist in seeking natural laws in such cases is as irrational as any primitive myth of the thunder gods. Science reveals consistent patterns that allow us to make negative statements about what natural forces cannot do.

Empirical evidence makes it clear that natural forces do not produce structures with high information content. This is not a statement about our *ignorance*—a "gap" in knowledge that will be filled in later by a natural explanation. Rather, it is a statement about what we *know*—about our consistent experience of the character of natural processes. Today, holding on to the hope that some natural process will be found to explain DNA is supremely irrational. The elusive process that naturalists hope to find would have to be completely unprecedented, different in kind from any we currently know. Surely *this* is an argument from ignorance.

When it comes to the origin of life, science is squarely on the side of creation by an intelligent agent. We have nothing to fear from the progress of science. And parents like Dave have solid answers to give their questioning teens.

DISCUSSION QUESTIONS

CHAPTER 3

1 If possible, at the beginning of the session dramatically wind up a one-hour oven timer as a way to open the discussion/ review of the two laws of thermodynamics. What are they? Why are they important?

2 Note the four ways naturalists tend to react to the reality of an "ultimate beginning." From your own experience, discuss examples of similar reactions when people are faced with truth.

3 Read aloud 2 Peter 3:3-9. Peter warns that mockers will deny God's promises by appealing to the stable course of nature. In what ways is this like the philosophy of naturalism?

4 According to verses 5 and 6, what do these mockers deliberately ignore to make their argument?

5 What do verses 7-9 suggest about why we are here during this time (while the "clock" is running down) when the gospel is being mocked and marginalized by naturalists?

6 There's a "nearly endless list of preconditions" on Earth that support human life. Start with those addressed in the text and add to the list from your observations of nature.

CHAPTER 4

7 Take the time to act out the following "letter" exercise and the Tinkertoy exercise if time and resources allow. They're not "just games"; it's easier to remember what we do than to remember what we read. A group leader should bring needed materials.

a. The group leader can bring a "sentence-full of letters." Depending on the size of your group and resources available, work with Scrabble letters, refrigerator letter magnets, letters cut out of construction paper, or large, bold letters printed from a computer. Choose letters that make a particular sentence. Start with the letters scrambled (on the floor, a table, or a magnetic board). Then unscramble the letters into the sensible sentence.

b. Pass out differing Tinkertoy or Lego pieces, six to ten per person in the group. Each represents an amino acid. Have each person "build" his or her own protein. Then consider the variety of "sculptures" the group has made. Compare this to the very particular links (and sequence) required to make a protein.

8. Discuss the limits of scientists' claims that they have recreated the building blocks of life and the ramifications in terms of intelligent cause.

9 "In everyday life, we weigh natural versus intelligent causes all the time without thinking much about it." Give examples from your own life. Some examples might be of "life with children." When a child says, "The dog did it," what makes you sure the dog wasn't responsible?

10 Make what social scientists call a "task analysis," determining exactly what and how many small steps are required to carry out a task or job. Start by scrambling your Scrabble letters from the exercise in question 7. Your "task" is to recreate the letters' sensible sentence. As you do so, identify and count *all* the steps in the task. Discuss how this is just a woefully inadequate illustration of the high information content of DNA.

11 George Washington Carver said, "I love to think of nature as an unlimited broadcasting system through which God speaks to us every hour, if we will only tune in." What natural

phenomenon have you seen, heard, tasted, smelled, or touched
this week that has testified to the reality of the Creator? (See
also Rom. 1:20.)

12 What examples of "bad science" have your children been
exposed to in school or in the media? Keep this discussion
in mind as you act out the role play—practicing ways to
persuasively and kindly counter these messages.

ROLE PLAY
Refer to the directions for role play, at the end of session 1
(pp. 27–28).

CONVERSATION STARTERS

a. One person takes the role of a Christian parent and the
other as a naturalist school teacher. Parent: Assume your
child was given the test question: "Where did Earth come
from?" The teacher marked as incorrect your child's answer:
"God." What could you say to the teacher that would "not
oppose science with religion" but would "oppose bad science
with better science"?

b. Assume a neighbor or teenager, like Katy, says to you,
"It's all just chemicals." The person role-playing the
naturalist should try to counter the Christian's points, to
help all participants hone arguments for intelligent design.

CLOSING SUMMARY
What is the most important point you want to remember from
this session?
Consider sharing this with the group.

DID WE "JUST EVOLVE"?

*As long as Darwinists control the
definitions of key terms [such as
science], their system is unbeatable,
regardless of the evidence.*

PHILLIP JOHNSON

CHAPTER 5

DARWIN IN THE DOCK

As you read, keep the following questions in mind:

- How have studies in animal breeding served to discredit Darwinian evolution?
- How do studies in gene mutations serve to discredit Darwinian evolution?
- How does the concept of irreducible complexity serve to discredit Darwinism?
- In the face of so much contradictory evidence, why do naturalistic scientists continue to hold on to Darwinism?

Since coming home from Disney World, Dave Mulholland had been conscientious in his search for answers. With the help of his pastor and several friends, he had found a handful of books that focused on the issues. He could now tell Katy what the big bang really means—how, instead of disproving that God created the world, the big bang theory actually gives scientific evidence for an ultimate beginning to the universe and points toward a transcendent source. He could put into words, without too much trouble, how the anthropic principle draws together overwhelming evidence for design running through the physical universe at every level. He could even field most of Katy's questions about where life came from—how laboratory experiments often "cheat" to get even the flimsiest results, and how the discovery of DNA gives positive evidence for a creator.

"Look, Katy," he had said to her. "Just think of your own experience. Have you ever seen a message written in the sky or on a rock by some kind of natural force?"

"Hmmm," she replied noncommittally.

Dave grabbed a book at random off his cluttered desk and flipped it open to a page of densely printed text. "Anyone who says some natural force in the chemicals 'wrote' the DNA code—well, that's like saying the chemicals in the paper and ink wrote the words on this page."

He was gaining confidence, and at times Katy dropped her defensive attitude and seemed genuinely interested in what he was learning. But today she was back to her old combative mode.

She tossed her head. "Oh, I don't have any problem with God being at the start of it all," she said airily. "Maybe he did kick everything off, you know, back at the very beginning."

Dave smiled inwardly. He knew this admission represented progress, even though Katy refused to show it.

"But everyone knows that once life was here, it evolved just as Darwin said it did. I saw it in my textbook at school."

It was her turn to grab a book. She rustled through her backpack and pulled out a heavy biology textbook, opening it to a full spread of colorful, eye-catching photos showing several breeds of dogs and horses as well as a vast variety of orchids and roses. Here, the caption proclaimed, is "evolution in action." Evolution happening before our very eyes.

Dave took the book from her hands and felt his stomach tighten. He hadn't covered these issues yet. And those colorful photos certainly were impressive.

Katy gazed at him triumphantly. "It's right in the book, Dad."

Dave didn't answer. His eyes had moved down to the text to find out exactly what his daughter was learning. Katy waited a few moments, then walked out of the room, leaving him sitting with the textbook still open on his lap. Dave clenched his hands. *God,* he prayed, *no wonder she keeps fighting me—fighting you. Everything she gets at school is saying that nature can do it on its own, that you are irrelevant.*

GOD THE IRRELEVANT

The tactic used in textbooks like Katy's is rarely a direct attack on religion. Instead, God is quietly but surely nudged into a position of irrelevance, where there's simply nothing left for him to do. Consider this typical example from the widely used college textbook *Evolutionary Biology:* "By coupling undirected, purposeless variation to the blind, uncaring process of natural selection, Darwin made theological or spiritual explanations of the life processes superfluous."[1]

The same message is aimed at high school students as well. In a 1995 statement, the National Association of Biology Teachers (NABT) asserted that all life is the outcome of "an unsupervised, impersonal, unpredictable, and natural process."[2] The words "unsupervised" and "impersonal" mean that God is not to be tolerated even in the role of directing and guiding the evolutionary process. Life is declared to be the outcome of material processes acting blindly by chance.

TRUE TO TYPE

Clearly, Katy's father is not the only one in a bind. All Christians need to know how to respond to the challenge posed by Darwinian naturalism. Fortunately, a few basic concepts will help us cut through the rhetoric and enable us to think more clearly. The best argument against Darwinism has been known for centuries by farmers and breeders, and it can be stated in a simple principle: Natural change in living things is limited. Or, stated positively: Organisms stay true to type.

Take the pictures in Katy's textbook. They tout the variation in
dogs and horses and roses as "evolution in action." The Darwinist
seems to overlook the obvious fact that the dogs are all still dogs,
the horses still horses, the roses still roses. None of the changes
has created a novel kind of organism. Dog breeding has given rise
to varieties ranging from the lumbering Great Dane to the tiny
Chihuahua, but no variety shows any tendency to leave the canine
family.

The magnificent Tyler Municipal Rose Garden in Tyler, Texas,
showcases some five hundred varieties of roses of nearly every
shade and hue. But despite intensive breeding, they are all still
roses. None of the examples cited in biology textbooks are evolving to a new level of complexity; they all simply illustrate variation
around a mean.

Darwinism cannot deny that all observed change is limited;
what the theory suggests is that over time, these minor variations
add up to create major changes—the vast changes necessary to go
from a primeval one-celled organism to bees and butterflies and
little boys.[3] This is the core of Darwinian theory—and yet, ironically, it is also the easiest part of the theory to discredit. Even
Charles Darwin's own work breeding pigeons demonstrates the
limits of biological change.

Darwin's Pigeons
In Victorian England, pigeon breeding was extremely popular,
and when Darwin returned from his famous sea voyage to the
Galapagos Islands, he took up pigeon breeding. In the skillful
hands of a breeder, the pigeon can be transformed into a fantail,
with feathers like a Chinese fan; it can become a pouter, with
a huge crop bulging under its beak; it can become a Jacobin,
with a "hood" of feathers on the back and sides of its head
resembling the hoods worn by Jacobin monks. Yet despite this
range of diversity, all pigeons are descendants of the common

rock pigeon, the ordinary gray birds that flock to our city parks.
And despite the spectacular variation in tails and feathers, all
the pigeons Darwin observed remained pigeons. They represent
cyclical change in gene frequencies but no new genetic information.

How did Darwin devise a theory of unlimited change from
such examples of limited change? He took the changes he had
observed and extrapolated them back into the distant past—which,
of course, he had *not* observed. If the common rock pigeon can be
so greatly transformed within a few years at the hand of a breeder,
he asked, what might happen to the same pigeon in nature over
thousands, even millions, of years? Given enough time, change
would be virtually unlimited, and the pigeon might even be transformed into a completely different kind of bird.[4]

It was a bold speculation, but no one should be misled into
thinking it was more than that. Neither Darwin nor anyone else
has ever actually witnessed evolution occurring. It is a conjecture,
an extrapolation going far beyond any observed facts. Now,
there's nothing wrong with extrapolation per se, as long as we
keep in mind that it is only that, not observable fact. And to
make a reasonable extrapolation, we must have good grounds
for believing that the process being extrapolated will continue
at a steady rate.

Limit That Cannot Be Crossed

And therein lies the fatal flaw in Darwin's theory. Centuries of
experiments show that the change produced by breeding does *not*
continue at a steady rate from generation to generation. Instead,
change is rapid at first, then levels off, and eventually reaches a
limit that breeders cannot cross.

Consider one historical example. Beginning in 1800, plant
breeders started trying to increase the sugar content of the sugar
beet, with excellent success. Over seventy-five years of selective

breeding, they increased the sugar content of beets from 6 percent to 17 percent. But then they could go no further. Although the same intensive breeding was continued for another half century, the sugar content never rose above 17 percent. At some point, biological variation always levels off and stops.

Why does progress halt? Because once all the genes for a particular trait have been selected, breeding can go no further. Breeding shuffles and selects among existing genes in the gene pool, combining and recombining them, much as you might shuffle and deal cards from a deck. But breeding does not create new genes, any more than shuffling cards creates new cards. A bird cannot be bred to grow fur. A mouse cannot be bred to grow feathers. A pig cannot grow wings.

What's more, as breeders keep up the selection pressure, the organism grows weaker until it finally becomes sterile and dies out. This is the bane of modern farming: Our highly bred cows and chickens produce more milk and eggs, but they are also much more prone to disease and sterility. There is a natural barrier that no amount of breeding is able to cross.

Moreover, when an organism is no longer subject to selective pressure, it tends to revert to its original type. Left to themselves, the offspring of the fancy pigeons that so charmed Darwin will revert to the wild rock pigeon.

So Darwin was simply mistaken in his extrapolation. Whether in the breeding pen or out in nature, the minor change produced by shuffling genes is not an engine for the unlimited change required by evolution. The natural tendency in living things is not to continue changing indefinitely but to stay close to the original type.

What About Mutations?
Since breeding does nothing more than shuffle existing genes, the only way to drive evolution to new levels of complexity is to

introduce new genetic material. And the only natural source
of new genetic material in nature is mutations. In today's neo-
Darwinism, the central mechanism for evolution is random
mutation and natural selection.

The concept of mutations was popularized for the younger set
a few years ago by the Teenage Mutant Ninja Turtles, and today
virtually every sci-fi movie features mutants. But what exactly is a
mutation? Since a gene is like a coded set of instructions, a mutation is akin to a typing error—a changed letter here, an altered
punctuation mark there, a phrase dropped, or a word misspelled.
These typing errors are the only source of novelty in the genetic
code.

But already there is an obvious problem. If you introduce a typing error into a report you are writing, it is not likely to improve
the report. An error is more likely to make nonsense than to make
better sense. And the same is true of errors in the genetic code.
Most mutations are harmful, often lethal, to the organism, so that
if mutations were to accumulate, the result would more likely be
*de*volution than evolution.

In order to make this theory work, neo-Darwinists must hope
that some mutations, somewhere, somehow, will be beneficial.
And since the evolution of a single new organ or structure may
require many thousands of mutations, neo-Darwinists must hope
that vast numbers of these rare beneficial mutations will occur in
a single organism. The improbabilities are staggering.

If we take neo-Darwinism into the laboratory and test it
experimentally, the difficulties only multiply. The handiest
way to study mutations in the laboratory is with the help of the
ordinary fruit fly—the kind you see hovering around overripe
bananas in the kitchen. Since this tiny fly reaches sexual maturity
in only five days, the effects of mutations can be observed over
several generations. Using chemicals or radiation to induce
mutations, scientists have produced flies with purple eyes or

white eyes; flies with oversized wings or shriveled wings or even
no wings; fly larvae with patchy bristles on their backs or larvae
with so many bristles that they resemble hedgehogs.[5]

But all this experimentation has not advanced evolutionary
theory in the slightest. For nothing has ever emerged except
odd forms of fruit flies. The experiments have never produced
a new type of insect. Mutations alter the details in *existing* structures—like eye color or wing size—but they do not lead to the
creation of *new* structures. The fruit flies have remained fruit
flies. Like breeding, genetic mutations produce only minor,
limited change.

Furthermore, the minor changes observed do not accumulate
to create major changes—the principle at the heart of Darwinism.
Hence, mutations are not the source of the endless, limitless
change required by evolutionary theory. Whether we look at
breeding experiments or laboratory experiments, the outcome
is the same: Change in living things remains strictly limited to
variations on the theme. We do not see the emergence of new
and more complex structures.

Fossil Verification

The same pattern holds throughout the past, as we see in the
fossil record. The overwhelming pattern is that organisms appear
fully formed, with variations clustered around a mean, and without transitional stages leading up to them. The fossil record as a
whole gives persuasive evidence against Darwinism.[6]

Cyclical Variations

Mastering these basic facts gives us the tools to think critically
about the examples typically used to support evolution. Take Darwin's famous finches, whose variation in beak size helped inspire
his initial theory. A recent study designed to support Darwinism
found that the finches' beaks grow larger in dry seasons, when the

seeds they eat are tough and hard, but grow smaller again after a rainy season, when tiny seeds become available once more. This is evolution happening "before [our] very eyes," the author of the study concluded. But in fact, it is precisely the opposite. The change in finch beaks is a cyclical fluctuation that allows the finches to adapt and survive, points out Phillip Johnson in *Reason in the Balance*. In other words, it's a minor adjustment that allows finches to . . . stay finches. It does not demonstrate that finches are evolving into a new kind of organism or that they originally evolved from another organism.[7]

Confirmation of Evolution?

The same holds for all the frequently cited "confirmations" of evolution, such as organisms that develop a resistance to antibiotics and insects that develop resistance to insecticide. Even more disturbing, some of the most famous examples have been exposed as hoaxes—most recently, the black-and-white peppered moths in England. Standard textbooks assert that during the Industrial Revolution, when the tree trunks were darkened by soot, a light-colored variety of the moth became easier for birds to see and were eaten up, while a darker moth flourished. This is touted as a classic illustration of natural selection, the theory that nature preserves those forms that function better than their rivals in the struggle for existence. But recently it was discovered that photographs showing the light moths against the darkened tree trunks were faked. Peppered moths fly about in the upper branches of trees and don't perch on the trunks at all. Even more recently, biologist Theodore Sargent of the University of Massachusetts admitted that he glued dead samples of the moths onto the tree trunks for a *NOVA* documentary. The respected journal *Nature* says the moth example, once the "prize horse in our stable" to illustrate evolution by natural selection, must now be thrown out.[8]

Reversion to the Average

No scientific finding has contradicted the basic principle that change in living things is limited. Luther Burbank, regarded as the greatest breeder of all time, said the tendency for organisms to stay true to type is so constant that it can be considered a natural law—what he called the law of the Reversion to the Average. It's a law, he said, that "keeps all living things within some more or less fixed limitations."[9]

Despite what the textbooks say, Darwin did not prove that nature is capable of crossing those "fixed limitations." He suggested only that it was theoretically possible—that minor changes might have accumulated over thousands of years until a fish became an amphibian, an amphibian became a reptile, and a reptile became a mammal. But after more than 150 years, it has become clear that Darwin's speculation flies in the face of all the results of breeding and laboratory experimentation, as well as the pattern in the fossil record.

The simple words from the first chapter of Genesis still stand firm: And God made every living thing to reproduce "after their kind" (see Gen. 1:11-12, 21, 24-25, NASB).

IRREDUCIBLE COMPLEXITY

The late Christian evangelist Francis Schaeffer used to offer an argument against evolution that was simple, easy to grasp, and devastating: Suppose a fish evolves lungs. What happens then? Does it move up to the next evolutionary stage?

Of course not. It drowns.

Living things cannot simply change piecemeal—a new organ here, a new limb there. An organism is an integrated system, and any isolated change in the system is more likely to be harmful than helpful. If a fish's gills were to begin mutating into a set of lungs, it would be a disaster, not an advantage. The only way to turn a fish into a land-dwelling animal is to transform it all at once, with a host of interrelated changes happening at the same time—not only lungs but also coadapted changes in the skeleton, the circulatory system, and so on.

The term to describe this kind of interdependent system is *irreducible complexity*. And the fact that organisms are irreducibly complex is yet another argument that they could not have evolved piecemeal, one step at a time, as Darwin proposed. Darwinian theory states that all living structures evolved in small, gradual steps from simpler structures—feathers from scales, wings from forelegs, blossoms from leaves, and so on. But <u>anything that is irreducibly complex cannot evolve in gradual steps, and thus its very existence refutes Darwin's theory.</u>

Consider the Mousetrap

The concept of irreducible complexity was developed by Michael Behe, a Lehigh University professor of biochemistry, in his 1993 book *Darwin's Black Box*. Behe's homey example of irreducible complexity is the mousetrap. A mousetrap cannot be assembled gradually, he points out. You cannot start with a wooden platform and catch a few mice, add a spring and catch a few more mice, add a hammer, and so on, each addition making the mousetrap function better. No, to even *start* catching mice, all the parts must be assembled from the outset. The mousetrap doesn't work until all its parts are present and working together.[10]

Many living structures are like the mousetrap. They involve an entire system of interacting parts all working together. If one part were to evolve in isolation, the entire system of interacting parts would stop functioning; and since, according to Darwinism, natural selection preserves the forms that function better than their rivals, the nonfunctioning system would be eliminated by natural selection—like the fish with lungs. Therefore, there is no possible Darwinian explanation of how irreducibly complex structures and systems came into existence.

Consider the Problem

Interestingly, Darwin himself grasped the problem and even admitted that it could falsify his theory. "If it could be demonstrated that any complex organ existed which could not possibly have been formed by numerous, successive, slight modifications," he wrote, "my theory would absolutely break down."[11] Today we can confidently say that his theory *has* broken down, for we now know that nature is full of examples of complex organs that could not possibly have been formed by numerous, slight modifications—that is, organs that are irreducibly complex.

Consider the Bat

Take the example of the bat. Evolutionists propose that the bat evolved from a small, mouselike creature whose forelimbs (the "front toes") developed into wings by gradual steps. But picture the steps: As the "front toes" grow longer and the skin begins to grow between them, the animal can no longer run without stumbling over them; and yet the forelimbs are not long enough to function as wings. And so, during most of its hypothetical transitional stages, the poor creature would have limbs too long for running and too short for flying. It would flop along helplessly and soon become extinct.

There is no conceivable pathway for bat wings to be formed in gradual stages. And this conclusion is confirmed by the fossil record, where we find no transitional fossils leading up to bats. The first time bats appear in the fossil record, they are already fully formed and virtually identical to modern bats.

Consider the Eye

A classic example of irreducible complexity is the human eye. An eye is no use at all unless all its parts are fully formed and working together. Even a slight alteration from its current form destroys its function. How, then, could the eye evolve by slight alterations?

Even in Darwin's day the complexity of the eye was offered as evidence against his theory, and Darwin said the mere thought of trying to explain the eye gave him "a cold shudder."

Darwin would have shuddered even harder had he known the structure of cells *inside* the eye. Contemporary Darwinists such as Richard Dawkins have tried to solve the problem by tracing a pathway to the evolution of the eye, starting with a light-sensitive spot, moving to a group of cells cupped to focus light better, and so on through a graded series of small improvements to produce a true lens. But as Behe points out, even the first step—the light-sensitive spot—is irreducibly complex, requiring a chain reaction of chemical reactions, starting when a photon interacts with a molecule called 11-*cis*-retinal, which changes to *trans*-retinal, which forces a change in the shape of a protein called rhodopsin, which sticks to another protein called transducin, which binds to another molecule . . . and so on. And where do those cupped cells that Dawkins talks about come from? There are dozens of complex proteins involved in maintaining cell shape, and dozens more that control groups of cells. Each of Dawkins's steps is itself a complex system, and adding them together doesn't answer where these complex systems came from in the first place. It's as if we asked how a stereo system is made, and someone answered, "By plugging a set of speakers into an amplifier and adding a CD player and a tape deck." Right. The real question is how to make those speakers and amplifiers in the first place.[12]

Consider a Single Cell

The most advanced, automated modern factory, with its computers and robots all coordinated on a precisely timed schedule, is less complex than the inner workings of a single cell. No such system could arise in a blind, step-by-step Darwinian process. The most rational explanation of irreducibly complex structures in nature is that they are products of the creative mind of an intelligent being.

THE REAL ISSUE

On all fronts, scientists are being forced to face up to the evidence for an intelligent cause. Ever since big bang theory was proposed, cosmologists have had to wrestle with the implications that the universe had an absolute beginning—and therefore a transcendent creator. The discovery of the information content in DNA is forcing biologists to recognize an intelligent cause for the origin of life. So, too, the fact of irreducible complexity is raising the question of design in living things.

Science cannot tell us everything we might wish to know about this intelligent cause, of course. It cannot reveal the details of God's character, and it cannot explain his plan of salvation. These are tasks for theology. But a study of the design and purpose in nature does clearly support the existence of a transcendent creator—so clearly that, as the apostle Paul writes in the New Testament, we stand before him without excuse (see Rom. 1:20).

Since the scientific evidence is so persuasive, why does the scientific establishment cling so tenaciously to Darwinian evolution? Why is Darwinism still the official creed in our public schools? Because the real issue is not what we see through the microscope or the telescope; it's what we adhere to in our hearts and minds. Darwinism functions as the cornerstone propping up a naturalistic worldview, and therefore the scientist who is committed to naturalism before he or she even walks into the laboratory is primed to accept even the flimsiest evidence supporting the theory. The most trivial change in living things is accepted as confirmation of the most far-flung claims of evolution, so that minor variation in finch beaks or insecticide resistance is touted as evidence that finches and flies both evolved ultimately from the slime by blind, unguided natural processes.

The core of the controversy is not science; it is a titanic struggle between opposing worldviews—between naturalism and theism. Is the universe governed by blind material forces or by a loving personal being? Only when Christians understand this— only when we clear away the smoke screens and get to the core issue—will we stop losing debates. Only then will we be able to help our kids, like Katy, face the continual challenges to their faith.

*Consider the situation of Christian
parents, not necessarily fundamen-
talists, who suspect that the term
evolution drips with atheistic
implications. The whole point of [the
more consistent Darwinists] is that
the parents are dead right about the
implications and the science educators
who deny this are either misinformed
or lying.* PHILLIP JOHNSON

CHAPTER 6

DARWIN'S DANGEROUS IDEA

As you read, keep the following questions in mind:
- What "non-scientific" areas of life does Darwinism threaten to subvert? How and why?
- What are the ramifications of Darwin's dangerous idea?
- What are the ramifications of our being uniquely created by a loving God?

Do evolution and religion really conflict? For public relations purposes many Darwinists veil their antagonism toward religion. For example, Harvard paleontologist Stephen J. Gould, though a prominent critic of design theory, insists he is not irreligious. Science and religion cannot conflict, he says, because they deal with different things: Science is about facts, while "religion struggles with human morality."[1]

Even many Christians have fallen for this tactic, with the result that we are often unprepared for the intellectual battles we face in a secular culture. For though Darwinism is a scientific theory and

must be answered with scientific evidence, it is more fundamentally a worldview—or, more precisely, a crucial plank in the
worldview of naturalism. And unless we engage it on that level,
we will remain ineffective in answering its challenges.

IMPLICATIONS OF DARWINISM

One evolutionist who is boldly up-front about this underlying
worldview is biologist William Provine of Cornell University. He
declares forthrightly that Darwinism is not just about mutations
and fossils; it is a comprehensive philosophy stating that all life
can be explained by natural causes acting randomly—which
implies that there is no need for the Creator. And if God did
not create the world, he notes, then the entire body of Christian
belief collapses.

Provine preaches his message on college campuses across the
country, often flashing the following list on an overhead projector
to hammer home what consistent Darwinism means: "No life
after death; no ultimate foundation for ethics; no ultimate meaning for life; no free will."[2] The only reason anyone still believes
in such things, Provine says, is that people have not yet grasped
the full implications of Darwinism.

His ideas may sound radical, but Provine is being brutally
honest. He recognizes that the biblical teaching of creation is not
just a theological doctrine; it is the very foundation of everything
Christians believe.

On the other side of the debate, Berkeley law professor Phillip
Johnson travels around the country arguing *against* Darwinism,
yet he agrees wholeheartedly with Provine on the far-reaching
implications of the theory. These implications often emerge when
Johnson speaks before secular audiences. As he writes, "I have
found that any discussion with modernists about the weaknesses
of the theory of evolution quickly turns into a discussion of poli-

tics, particularly sexual politics." Why? Because modernists "typically fear that any discrediting of naturalistic evolution will end in
women being sent to the kitchen, gays to the closet, and abortion-
ists to jail."[3]

In other words, most people sense instinctively that there is
much more at stake here than a scientific theory—that a link
exists between the material order and the moral order. Though
the fears Johnson encounters are certainly exaggerated, this basic
intuition is right. Our origin determines our destiny. It tells us
who we are, why we are here, and how we should order our lives
together in society. Our view of origins shapes our understanding
of ethics, law, education—and yes, even sexuality. Whether we
start with the assumption that we are creatures of a personal
God or that we are products of a mindless process, a whole network of consequences follows, and these consequences diverge
dramatically.

Ethical Implications

Take ethics. If a transcendent God created us for a purpose, then
the most rational approach is to ask, What is that purpose, and
how must we live in order to fulfill it? The answer is found in
divine revelation; its moral commands tell us how we can become
the people God created us to be. So Christian morality is not
subjective, based on our personal feelings; it is objective, based
on the way God created human nature. Skeptics often dismiss
Christianity as "irrational," but if we were indeed created, then
the truly irrational course is to ignore the Creator's moral rules.

By contrast, naturalism claims that God did not create us;
rather, it is we who created the idea of God. He "exists" only
in the minds of those who believe in him. If this claim is true,
then the most rational course is to dismiss religion as wishful
thinking and to base morality squarely on what is real—on scientific knowledge. And science tells us that humans are products of

evolutionary forces, that morality is nothing more than an idea
that appears in our minds when we have evolved to a certain level.
Consequently, there is no ultimate objective basis for morality;
humans create their own standards. Since the only objective reality
that exists is the natural world, and it is in constant evolutionary
flux, our ideas about right and wrong are constantly changing as
well. The result is radical ethical relativism.

Legal Implications

Or consider the subject of law. Traditionally, a nation's laws were
understood to be based on a transcendent moral order (based in
turn on divine law). The belief was that "men do not make laws.
They do but discover them. Laws . . . must rest on the eternal
foundation of righteousness." These words may sound as if they
came from the pen of a sixteenth-century divine, but they were
written in the early twentieth century by our thirtieth president,
Calvin Coolidge.[4]

Yet if Darwinism is true, there is no divine law or transcendent
moral order, and there is no final, authoritative basis for law.
The influential legal theorist Oliver Wendell Holmes, an avowed
Darwinian, taught that laws are merely a codification of political
policies judged to be socially and economically advantageous.
Law is reduced to a managerial skill used in the service of social
engineering—the dominant view in the legal profession today.

Educational Implications

In education, Darwinism has molded not only the content but also
the methodology of teaching. The key figure is John Dewey, who
sought to work out what Darwinism means for the learning process. If human beings are part of nature and nothing more, he
reasoned, then the mind is simply an organ that has evolved from
lower forms in the struggle for existence—just as wings or claws
have evolved—and its value depends on whether it works, whether

it enables the organism to survive. Dewey rejected the traditional belief that an idea is an insight into an objective reality, to be judged by whether it is true or false. Instead, he argued that ideas are merely hypotheses about what will get the results we want, and their validity depends on whether they work. Dewey's pragmatic philosophy is the source of much of the relativism that has gutted both academic and moral education today.

Darwinism is even a key source of postmodernism, which dismisses the idea of universal truth as a tool of oppression wielded by "Dead White Males." Because Darwinism eliminates the transcendent, postmodernism draws the inevitable conclusion that there is no transcendent truth. Each of us is locked in the limited perspective of our race, gender, and ethnic group. The "search for truth" that supposedly motivates education is a sham; there is only the black perspective, the feminist perspective, the Hispanic perspective, and so on. Any claim to universal truth is considered an attempt to impose the perspective of one group on all the others.

Despite its flamboyant skepticism toward objective truth, ironically, postmodernism rests on an assumption that *something* is objectively true—namely, Darwinism.

If tying Darwinism to postmodernism seems a bit of a stretch, listen to the personal odyssey of the influential postmodernist guru Richard Rorty, now at Stanford University. In an autobiographical essay, Rorty reveals that he was once attracted to Christianity. But finding himself "incapable" of "the humility that Christianity demanded," he turned away from God—only to discover that a world without God is a world without any basis for universal truth or justice.[5] Rorty then determined to work out a philosophy consistent with Darwinism. Like Dewey, he accepted the Darwinist notion that ideas are problem-solving tools that evolve as means of adapting to the environment. "Keeping faith with Darwin," Rorty writes, means understanding that the human species is not oriented "toward Truth," but only

"toward its own increased prosperity."[6] Truth claims are just
tools that "help us get what we want."[7] (Which means, of course,
that Rorty's own ideas are just tools for getting what *he* wants—
including the idea of postmodernism. Thus, postmodernism
refutes itself.)

Darwinism thus forms the linchpin to the fundamental debate
between Christianity and naturalism in virtually every subject area.
Since modern culture has given science authority to define the
way the world "really is," Darwinism provides the scientific justifi-
cation for a naturalistic approach in every field. As British biologist Richard Dawkins puts it, Darwin "made it possible to be
an intellectually fulfilled atheist."[8]

DARWIN'S FIRST COMMITMENT

Many Christians shrink from drawing such a stark contrast
between theism and Darwinism. They hope to combine Darwin's
biological theory with belief in God—suggesting that God may
have used evolution as his method of creating. Yet Darwin himself
insisted that the two are mutually exclusive.[9] For natural selection
acts as a sieve, sifting out harmful variations in living things and
preserving helpful variations. But if God were guiding evolution,
he would ensure that each variation was beneficial from the start.
Natural selection would be, in Darwin's own words, "superfluous."[10] The whole point of his theory was to identify a natural
process that would mimic intelligent design, thus making *design*
superfluous.

Darwin is typically portrayed as a man forced to the theory of
natural selection by the weight of the facts. But today historians
recognize that he was first committed to the philosophy of naturalism and then sought a theory to justify it scientifically. Early in
his career, he had already turned against the idea of creation and
developed a settled conviction that, as he put it, "Everything in

nature is the result of fixed laws."[11] In other words, the deck was already stacked in favor of a naturalistic account of life before he actually uncovered any convincing facts.

Indeed, nature became virtually a substitute deity for Darwin. "As regards his respect for the laws of Nature," wrote his son William, "it might be called reverence if not a religious feeling. No man could feel more intensely the vastness and the inviolability of the laws of nature."[12] With his attitude akin to religious worship, it is not surprising that Charles Darwin eventually attributed godlike creative powers to natural selection.

Modern Darwinists insist that evolution is so obviously supported by the facts that anyone who dissents must be ignorant or dishonest. But Darwin was more candid. He knew quite well he had not proved his theory of natural selection. He described it as an inference, grounded chiefly on analogy. It can be judged only by how useful it is, he wrote, how well "it groups and explains phenomena."[13]

Supporters Saw Weakness

Likewise, many of Darwin's earliest and most ardent supporters were quick to spot the scientific weaknesses in his theory, yet they chose to champion it because they saw it as a useful means of promoting naturalistic philosophy. Herbert Spencer, the first person to extend evolution into every discipline, from ethics to psychology, explained frankly that he felt an enormous internal pressure to find a naturalistic alternative to the idea of creation. "The Special Creation belief had dropped out of my mind many years before," he wrote, "and I could not remain in a suspended state: acceptance of the only conceivable alternative was peremptory." Moreover, Spencer admitted, once you accept the philosophy of naturalism, some form of naturalistic evolution is an "inevitable corollary"—regardless of the strength of the scientific evidence.[14]

Thomas Huxley christened himself "Darwin's bulldog" and fought fiercely for the cause, and yet by his own admission, he never thought Darwin's theory amounted to much scientifically. He, too, rallied to the cause for philosophical reasons. Long before his encounter with Darwin, Huxley had rejected the biblical teaching of creation and was actively looking for an alternative. Huxley declared that Darwin "did the immense service of freeing us forever from the dilemma—Refuse to accept the creation hypothesis, and what have you to propose that can be accepted by any cautious reasoner?"[15] Apparently Huxley was willing to champion *any* naturalistic theory, even one he found scientifically flawed, as long as it provided an alternative to creation.

The historical data makes it clear that the contest over evolution in the nineteenth century was philosophically "rigged." Darwinism won not so much because it fit the evidence but because it provided a scientific rationale for naturalism. If the world is governed by uniformly operating laws, as Huxley said, then the successive populations of beings "must have proceeded from one another in the way of progressive modification."[16] The operative word here is "must." Once you accept philosophical naturalism, then something very much like Darwinism *must* be true—regardless of the facts.

Darwin's early opponents likewise understood what was at stake. In 1874, Princeton theologian Charles Hodge published an essay asking "What Is Darwinism?" And he answered bluntly that it is tantamount to atheism. "Natural selection is selection made by natural laws, working without intention and design," Hodge wrote. And "the denial of design in nature is virtually the denial of God."[17]

In our own day, one of the most explicit statements of the philosophical motivation behind Darwinism comes, surprisingly enough, from Harvard geneticist Richard Lewontin. In an article arguing for the superiority of science over religion (which he groups with things like UFOs and channeling), Lewontin freely admits that science has its own problems. It has created many of our social problems (like ecological disasters), and many scientific theories are no more than "unsubstantiated just-so stories." Nevertheless, "in the struggle between science and the supernatural," we "take the side of science." Why? "Because we have a prior commitment to materialism."[18]

An Honest Debate

Note carefully those last few words. Lewontin is admitting that the hostility to religion that is fashionable in the scientific establishment is not driven by the facts but by materialistic philosophy.

And there is more, for Lewontin says even the methods of science are driven by materialistic philosophy. The rules that define what qualifies as science in the first place have been crafted by materialists in such a way as to ensure they get only materialistic theories. Or, as Lewontin puts it, "we are forced by our *a priori* adherence to material causes to create an apparatus of investigation and a set of concepts that produce material explanations."[19]

This is a stunning admission. The authority of science rests primarily on its public image—on the impression that its theories rest firmly on a foundation of empirical facts. But Lewontin has pulled back the curtains in Oz to reveal the wizard's strings and levers. The truth is that much of Darwinism is not science but naturalistic philosophy masquerading as science. So an honest debate between Darwinism and Christianity is not fact versus faith but philosophy versus philosophy, worldview versus worldview.

We must be clear about what is at stake here. As long as Darwinism reigns in our schools and elite culture, the Christian worldview will be considered the madwoman in the attic—irrational and unbelievable. That's why we can no longer allow

naturalists to treat science as a sanctuary where their personal
philosophy reigns free from challenge.

WHO IS "THIS GUY"?

In William Steig's *Yellow & Pink,* a delightfully whimsical picture
book for children, two wooden figures wake up to find themselves
lying on an old newspaper in the hot sun. One figure is painted
yellow, the other pink.

Suddenly, Yellow sits up and asks, "Do you know what we're
doing here?"

"No," replies Pink. "I don't even remember getting here."

So begins a debate between the two marionettes over the origin
of their existence.

Pink surveys their well-formed features and concludes, "Someone must have made us."

Yellow disagrees. "I say we're an accident," and he outlines a
hypothetical scenario of how it might have happened. A branch
might have broken off a tree and fallen on a sharp rock, splitting
one end of the branch into two legs. Then the wind might have
sent it tumbling down a hill until it was chipped and shaped. Perhaps a flash of lightning struck in such a way as to splinter the
wood into arms and fingers. Eyes might have been formed by
woodpeckers boring in the wood.

"With enough time, a thousand, a million, maybe two and
a half million years, lots of unusual things could happen," says
Yellow. "Why not us?"

The two figures argue back and forth.

In the end, the discussion is cut off by the appearance of a man
coming out of a nearby house. He strolls over to the marionettes,
picks them up, and checks their paint. "Nice and dry," he comments, and tucking them under his arm, he heads back toward the
house.

Peering out from under the man's arm, Yellow whispers in
Pink's ear, "Who is this guy?"[20]

GOD GIVES MEANING

That is precisely the question each one of us must answer, and
it's no storybook fantasy. It is deadly serious. Beyond the public
debates and rhetoric, beyond the placard waving and politicizing,
at the heart of every worldview are the intensely personal questions: Who made me, and why am I here?

Every worldview has to begin somewhere—God or matter,
take your choice. Everything else flows from that initial choice.
This is why the question of creation has become such a fierce
battleground today. It is the foundation of the entire Christian
worldview. For <u>if God created all of finite reality, then every</u>
<u>aspect of that reality must be subject to him and his truth. Every-</u>
<u>thing finds its meaning and interpretation in relation to God.</u>
No part of life can be autonomous or neutral, no part can be sliced
off and made independent from Christian truth. Because creation
includes the whole scope of finite reality, the Christian worldview
must be equally comprehensive, covering every aspect of our lives,
our thinking, our choices. Both friends and foes of Christianity
realize that everything stands or falls on the doctrine of creation.

BEGIN WITH BEGINNINGS

Christians often seek to evangelize others by starting with salvation—John 3:16 and the gospel message. And for an earlier generation, that approach worked. Most people had some kind of
church experience in their background, even if they did not have
strong personal beliefs. But in today's post-Christian world, many
people no longer even understand the meaning of crucial biblical
terms. For example, the basic term *sin* makes no sense to people if

they have no concept of a holy God who created us and who therefore has a right to require certain things of us. And if people don't understand sin, they certainly don't comprehend the need for salvation.

Consequently, in today's world, beginning evangelism with the message of salvation is like starting a book at the middle—you don't know the characters, and you can't make sense of the plot. Instead, we must begin with Genesis, where the main character, God, establishes himself as the Creator, and the "plot" of human history unfolds its first crucial episodes. And the scientific evidence supporting these opening episodes is powerful, as Dave Mulholland discovered in his personal odyssey.

First, cosmology has discovered the shattering truth that matter is not eternal after all, as naturalistic scientists once confidently assumed. The universe began at a finite period of time—which in turn implies that something *outside* the universe must have set it going.

Second, there are the staggering "coincidences" that make the universe fit for life. From the molecular properties of water to the balance of electrical charges in the proton and electron, the entire structure of the physical universe is exquisitely designed to support life on Earth.

Third, laboratory experiments touted as proof that life can arise spontaneously by random natural forces turn out to prove nothing of the sort. Instead, they provide positive evidence that life can be created only by an intelligent agent controlling, directing, and manipulating the process. The discovery of DNA gives explosive new force to the argument for design. If we rely on experience— and, after all, science is *supposed* to be based on experience—the only known source of information is an intelligent cause.

Fourth, Darwin did not succeed in demonstrating that life developed by means of mindless, undirected natural forces. Experiments with breeding and mutations have shown that his fundamental assumption—that living things can vary endlessly—is fatally flawed. Today, the most advanced investigations into the heart of the cell confirm that the irreducible complexity of living things can be explained only by intelligent design.

The continued dominance of Darwinism has less to do with its scientific validity than with a commitment to naturalism. Naturalism, in turn, has spread like a toxic oil spill into fields as diverse as ethics, law, education, postmodernism—to name just a few. As a result, Darwinism has become the cornerstone for a comprehensive philosophy that stands in stark opposition to Christianity.

ROAD MAP TO REALITY

Every worldview is a proposed map of reality, a guide to navigating in the world. One effective test of any truth claim, therefore, is to ask whether we can live by it. If you follow a map but still find yourself splashing into rivers or crashing off cliffs, you can be quite sure something is wrong with the map. By the same token, if you live according to a certain worldview but keep bumping up against reality in painful ways, you can be sure something is wrong with the worldview. It fails to reflect reality accurately.

Let's apply this test to the naturalistic worldview of the well-known science popularizer Carl Sagan, whom we have referred to several times in this section. Sagan literally canonized the cosmos, openly plugging his personal philosophy on his popular television program. And far from repudiating this transformation of science into religion, the scientific establishment richly rewarded him, even awarding him the National Academy of Science's Public Welfare Medal in 1994.

One consequence of Sagan's religion of the cosmos was that he was actively committed to the cause of animal rights. And quite logically so. For if humans evolved from the beasts, there can be no intrinsic difference between them. It would be just as cruel and immoral to kill a cow as to murder a person. "In my writings," Sagan said in a *Parade* magazine article, "I have tried to show how closely related we are to other animals, how cruel it is to gratuitously inflict pain on them."[21] As a result, he was adamantly opposed to using animals for medical research. For if animals have the same value as humans, how can we justify expending their lives to save humans?

But on this issue, Sagan bumped up against reality in a very painful way. In 1994, he discovered that he had myelodysplasia, a rare blood disease. With possibly just months to live, he was told that his only chance for survival was an experimental bone-marrow transplant. But there was one catch: The procedure that might save his life had been developed by research on animals— the kind of research Sagan passionately opposed.

Sagan faced an excruciating dilemma: Should he remain true to his naturalistic philosophy and reject the marrow graft as some-thing acquired by immoral means? Or should he agree to undergo the medical treatment in hope of saving his life, though it meant acting in contradiction to his moral convictions?

Sagan didn't take long to reach a decision: He underwent three bone-marrow treatments, which did extend his life for a time (though he ultimately succumbed to the disease and died in 1996). At the time Sagan wrote the *Parade* article, he was still, in his words, "very conflicted" over the choice he had made. He recog-nized clearly that his decision to accept the treatment was a practi-cal denial of his naturalistic worldview. But when he came up against reality, he abandoned his naturalistic road map and, whether he admitted it or not, implicitly shifted to the biblical road map, which says that humans do have a value transcending that of plants and animals.

Christianity is not merely a religion, defined narrowly as per-sonal piety and corporate worship. It is also an objective perspec-tive on all reality, a complete worldview. Only Christianity consistently stands up to the test of practical living. Only Christianity gives us an accurate road map. Only Christianity matches the way we must act if we are to live humanely and rationally in the real world.

Creation is the first element of the Christian worldview, the foundation on which everything else is built. It is the basis of human dignity, for our origin tells us who we are, why we are here, and how we should treat one another. The questions of human life have become the most pressing issues of our day, as two men discovered in a very personal way on a battlefield on the other side of the globe.

SESSION 3

DISCUSSION QUESTIONS

CHAPTER 5

1 How have studies in animal breeding actually served to discredit, rather than justify, Darwinian evolution?

2 What fatal flaws are at the heart of Darwin's theory? What truth remains firm, as found in Genesis 1:11-25?

3 As a group, look at a spring mousetrap. Take it apart, if possible, to clearly grasp the impossibility of it serving its function if it were only partially assembled. Brainstorm to name other objects, besides a mousetrap, that illustrate the principle of irreducible complexity. How does the concept of irreducible complexity serve to discredit Darwinian evolution?

4 In the face of so much contradictory evidence, why do naturalistic scientists continue to hold on to Darwinism?

CHAPTER 6

5 Discuss contrasting ramifications of a naturalist worldview and a Christian worldview in regard to the following:

a. ethics

b. the nature and purpose of law

c. educational content and theory

6 Read aloud Acts 17:16-34. The best way of combating the religion of science is by defeating it on its own turf, then bringing the gospel and the Word of God into the void that has been created. This is a biblical strategy, which can be seen from observing how the apostle Paul addressed citizens of Athens. In verses 16-18, how would you describe Paul's manner of speech among the Athenians? What does this say to you as you approach naturalists?

7 On Mars Hill, on what point did Paul begin his persuasive presentation (vv. 22-23)? As important as the clear gospel message is, why might "sin and salvation" not be a good starting point for discussions with a naturalist? On what point might you start a discussion?

8 What steps did Paul take to get from his observation about their gods (v. 22) to the proclamation of coming judgment and the resurrection of Christ (v. 31)?

9 If your persuasive conversations with naturalists mirror the Mars Hill presentation of Paul, what three reactions might you expect? Faced with each reaction, how would you respond or follow up?

10 In what specific ways can members of the group support and help one another in countering "bad science" presented to your children or neighbors?

ROLE PLAY

Refer to the directions for role play, at the end of session 1 (pp. 27–28).

CONVERSATION STARTERS

a. One person can take the role of a parent, the other person take the role of a skeptical teen. Assume the teen, like Katy, says, "But everyone knows that once life was here, it evolved, one species to another. I saw it in my textbook at school."

b. To review the four major points in the case for creation and design, assume one person is a contemporary apostle Paul, presenting a case for Christian faith to a small group of naturalists informally meeting at a coffee bar. Have this role play clearly be a dialogue, not a "sermon."

CLOSING SUMMARY

What is the most important point you want to remember from this session?

Consider sharing this with the group.

CHOOSE LIFE

A MATTER OF LIFE

As you read, keep the following questions in mind:
- In what ways did God show his mercy and grace to Ken McGarity?
- How did Ken finally come to realize that mercy and grace?

VIETNAM, 1968

From their hovering position fifteen hundred feet above the ground, the men in Colonel Yarborough's Command & Control (C&C) helicopter kept watch at the end of an anxious day. For the past two weeks, their Ghostrider division had been shuttling in troops and supplies for a big push in the central highlands at Plei Merong. The atmosphere was tense, the territory unsecured. During reconnaissance, as Yarborough's crew had hovered over the area for the first time, they had spotted a stockpile of empty rocket crates not more than three hundred yards from the present landing zone. The enemy could be anywhere.

As the C&C copter circled slowly over the jungle, the crew watched another helicopter rotor into position above the steep hillside landing zone, hovering close to the ground to pick up support personnel returning to base. The men on the C&C copter could see men scurrying below, disappearing in and out of the scrub trees and bushes. The mechanical dragonfly wigwagged, impatient to leave.

Kaboom!

Suddenly the air burst with rockets. Puffs of white smoke from small firearms rose in dozens of places over the hillside. The copter near the ground recoiled left, as if stabbed in its side. A curling plume of gray scorpioned the back rotor, and the machine began to pitch wildly. The smoke grew black and full.

As the wounded machine continued to yaw and heave, Ken McGarity watched the scene from his right-gunner position in the C&C copter. He saw the other helicopter fall, slamming down onto the landing zone, its main rotor shattering. He spotted two helmets pop out. Then another. The three men ran for cover, one of them on fire.

The black smoke from the hit copter mushroomed, obscuring Ken's view. Rockets continued to shoot up through the smoke, though they didn't have the range to reach the C&C copter.

"We're going down!" screamed the C&C pilot. He shouted and waved at Ken to watch his side as they spiraled down.

Ken took his gun off its stand and knelt in the doorway, his right foot out on the skid. He leaned out as far as he could, straining to see. He had to know where their own men were before he could lay down a blanket of fire.

The colonel pushed his way to the open door, beside Ken, ready to throw out an extinguisher for the burning soldier on the ground. Their C&C copter had cleared the high bamboo and would soon be down to the scrub trees, but Ken still couldn't see where their guys were hiding. He couldn't see the enemy either.

Soon they were right over the landing zone. Why didn't the colonel throw out the extinguisher? They weren't supposed to be here more than seven seconds. They had been here at least twenty. *Throw the thing!*

No one saw the B-40 rocket coming.

Half the ship exploded on contact. Ken was catapulted into

the air and fell from the height of the scrub trees onto the bare ground. . . .

When he regained consciousness, Otto Mertz, a buddy from the first downed copter, was dragging him through the mud to safety.

"My legs!" Ken screamed.

"They're broken," someone said.

His arms had been crossed over his chest. *They must be broken, too,* Ken thought.

He passed in and out of consciousness several times before he was finally hoisted onto a medevac helicopter. When he was secured into a transport stretcher, a woman's voice asked, "What's your name?"

"McGarity," he said. "Ken McGarity. Am I hurt bad?"

"We're going to take care of you," the nurse shouted as the thrashing blades lifted them away.[1]

"IT'S NOT UP TO ME"

When the wounded men arrived at the Army's 71st Evacuation Hospital at Pleiku on September 21, 1968, Dr. Kenneth Swan was surgeon of the day. The thirty-three-year-old doctor had been in Vietnam only a month.

Two men had died at Plei Merong. All the others could be classified as "walking wounded," having sustained only minor injuries—all except the soldier identified as Army Specialist 4 Ken McGarity. The man was covered with dirt and bloodied mud. One leg hung by a thin strip of skin; the other was broken so badly that the femur protruded from what was left of his thigh. Shoelace tourniquets had stopped the arterial bleeding, but the wounds were plastered with mud and sticks. Both arms were badly fractured and pitted with shrapnel wounds. The man's right pinkie finger was gone, and one testicle had been blown away. Blood oozed from both eyes, and the left eyeball was shattered. The injuries to the eyes indicated shrapnel wounds, which could mean brain damage.

As Swan assessed the devastation before him, he had two choices. He could classify the soldier as "expectant," medicate him, and leave him to die, or he could devote the full resources of the hospital to treating him. Which call should he make?

By all rights, this soldier should have bled to death already. He had been in the field almost two hours before being airlifted out. But he was not only alive, he was conscious.

"How am I doing?" the man asked.

"You're in the hospital."

"I feel like I left my legs back on the helicopter. They're broken, aren't they?"

Dr. Swan knew the soldier's joke was closer to the truth, but the short exchange helped Swan make up his mind. As a Christian, how could he refuse to treat a man who was talking to him?

"We're going to take care of you," he promised.

X rays revealed what the surgeon already knew: The soldier's legs had to come off. As Swan worked on the amputations—both legs above the knee—he coordinated the activities of the team of doctors he had called in. The orthopedist treated the shrapnel wounds in McGarity's arms. The ophthalmologist removed the man's left eye and cleaned the wounds to the right eye, hoping to save it. When the orthopedist had done all he could on McGarity's arms, Swan amputated the ragged stump of the soldier's right pinkie finger. A urologist worked to limit the damage of the "shrapnel vasectomy."

Then, in a final delicate and involved surgery, the neurologist performed a craniotomy, cutting through the top of the soldier's forehead and lifting away the skull so that he could extract the shrapnel from the brain's frontal lobes—damage that might have a lobotomizing effect. Or worse.

For eight hours, the surgeons stood in their muddy boots on the concrete floor and did the best they could to repair Ken McGarity. A civilian photographer from Casualty Care hovered about—much to the surgeons' irritation—recording the soldier's wounds for a research study. In the background, providing a bizarre rhythmic accompaniment, the adjacent air base took incoming mortar fire.

When the surgeries were completed, Dr. Swan felt his team had done well. Their patient had a chance.

The next morning, however, Swan's commanding officer sat down with him in the mess hall and grilled him about the case. Why had he decided to treat the recent casualty so aggressively?

"There was no other way to treat his injuries," Swan replied, surprised at the question.

His superior looked him squarely in the eye. "Look, Ken, why send blind, double amputees with significant brain damage back to their parents? What were you thinking?"

Swan found himself responding from his gut. "I was trained to *treat* the sick. It's not up to me who lives and dies. That's God's decision."

"As the surgeon on duty, it *was* up to you," said his commanding officer. "The next time you make a call, ask yourself what kind of life you're condemning someone to." He paused. "Of course, he may die yet." He sounded grimly hopeful.

"I'M ALIVE"

Several days later, Rick Martin, a fellow enlistee from Alabama, stopped in the ICU to visit Ken McGarity. His friend's head was swathed in a giant bandage. His broken arms were restrained in tight wraps that allowed their wounds to be freshly dressed. A single sheet covered his bandaged leg stumps, each of which had swollen to the size of his waist.

"Hey, buddy," he said. "It's Rick Martin."

"Look at this, man—my legs are broke. My eyes must have got sandblasted, too."

The nurse had told Rick that Ken did not yet understand the severity of his injuries. But hearing how wrong Ken's impressions were, Rick became distraught, almost angry. Someone had to tell the guy the truth.

"No, man," Rick said. He paused a moment, gathering courage. "Your legs aren't broke. They were amputated."

"Really?"

"Yeah. You lost your legs."

"How about my eyes?"

"I'm sorry. You're going to be blind."

"My arms feel like they're there."

"Yeah, your arms are going to be okay. They're just broken."

Ken was silent for so long that Rick wondered if the drugs had lulled him back to sleep.

"Okay, then," Ken said finally. "Okay."

Rick didn't know what to make of his friend's resignation; he figured it was probably the morphine talking.

"I want you to do something for me, Rick," Ken said. "I really need you to do this. Write my mom and dad and tell them that I got my legs broken and that sand blew in my eyes. But tell them I'm going to be all right. I don't want them to know how bad it is. Will you do that?"

"Sure," said Rick. "Sure."

"You got a cigarette, man?" Ken asked.

"Yeah," he said, "but I don't think we'd better light up in here with all this oxygen around. We'll probably blow the place up."

"Get me out of here then," Ken said.

"I'm not sure—"

"Just load me in a wheelchair and take me out."

Rick scooped Ken up. The guy felt as light and frail as Rick's nine-year-old brother.

Outside, on the hardpan ground surrounding the ICU, Ken tilted his head back and took deep breaths.

"Feel that, Rick?" he asked. "Feel the wind? It feels good on my face."

Rick lit a cigarette and put it in Ken's mouth. He took a couple drags, then Rick took the cigarette back.

"I'm alive," Ken said.

"You're darn right," said Rick, starting to feel an odd glimmer of enthusiasm. "You're smoking."

"The wind feels good," Ken said again. He took a full breath. Then another. Then a shuddering came over him. "I'm going to pass out now, Rick."

"Okay. I've got you, buddy."

GOOD NEWS OR BAD?

A month later, the chaplain's assistant, another young man from Ken McGarity's hometown of Phenix City, Alabama, brought Dr. Kenneth Swan a piece of news. "Thought you would like to know, McGarity made it back. He's at Walter Reed."

Kenneth Swan should have been happy to hear those words, but he was not. He envisioned the damaged soldier living in a veterans hospital, heavily medicated against the violent rages or psychotic delusions brought on by brain damage. He saw the man half-curled in a wheelchair, stretching his neck and muttering in a drugged rage. These images burned in the surgeon's imagination, where they would remain for twenty years.

TALKING TO GOD

By the time Ken McGarity reached Walter Reed Army Medical Center in Washington, D.C., three weeks after being wounded, the nightmares had started. As additional surgeries were performed to repair the ligament damage in his right arm and his amputation wounds, pain exploded at every level of his consciousness.

In his dreams he saw North Vietnamese regulars running down the middle of the base's airstrip. . . . The bodies were being picked up after Tet. . . . He leaned out of the copter once more, desperate to identify his own men. . . . He was running down a road in the middle of a firefight wearing only a T-shirt, fatigues, and boots. "Never go anywhere without your weapon!" his sergeant barked. "Never!" A rocket exploded, and he woke screaming, covered with sweat.

The nurse whispered, "We let you sleep through your last meds. We won't do that again." She gave him another shot of morphine.

He wanted to tell her that he was afraid to sleep. Then the morphine took over once more.

In McGarity's rare moments of lucidity, something else scared him—as much or more than his nightmares, though in a completely different way. When he had re-upped for his second tour in Vietnam, requesting reassignment to helicopter duty from his relatively safe post in the 75th Engineering Battalion, he had gone home for a month's leave. While there, one evening he drove out by the lake to be alone with his thoughts.

At first he relaxed, lying back in the long grass, watching the stars come out. But soon the sky's immensity seemed to tilt, levering until it threatened to topple on him. Suddenly he was straining to breathe against a pressing sense of fear.

What was he afraid of?

Death.

That was the thought smothering him. He didn't want to die. Anything but that. He was too young to leave this world that he was just beginning to discover.

He sat up, as if throwing open his own coffin, and lifted his arms up to the skies. "God, if you are there and will be with me, let me know," he prayed. "Give me a sign."

What sign?

In an instant, he made the deal. "You can take my eyes, you can take my arms, my legs, my mind, but leave my life." Did he know what he was offering? He thought he did. Suffering didn't scare him. Death did.

So when Rick Martin had first told Ken that he had lost his legs and his sight, Ken's mind had instantly flashed back to that deal he'd made with God. When he had said okay to Rick, it was really God that Ken had been talking to.

Now, lying in Walter Reed Army Medical Center, it was clear that God was real. God had heard him and had taken almost everything he had offered—but had left him his life. Even in the midst of his living nightmare, Ken McGarity realized that his life was a gift from God. God had not taken his life. *Why not? And where do I go from here? What does God want from me?*

NO PAY FOR PITY

When Ken arrived at Hines Veterans Administration Hospital outside Chicago to begin his rehabilitation on the blind ward, orderlies wheeled his eighty-pound body into the hospital. In transport, he had sweated out every toxin his infection-riddled body could produce.

"He sure needs to be cleaned up," said the nurse during his intake.

"I don't know what I'm supposed to do with him," complained the psychiatrist. "Why didn't they let this guy die?"

Why did people assume that because he was blind he was also deaf, Ken wondered. They not only spoke past him, they talked as if saving his life had been a mistake.

On the blind ward at Hines, however, Ken discovered a new power. He didn't have to do anything he didn't want to do. He had always been independent to a fault. Now he could play out his rebellion with abandon.

Medical personnel told him he needed to begin learning how to live his new life. He needed to exercise his arms, develop his upper body strength. But Ken only wanted the pain to go away. So he decided he would just lie in his bed and let them take care of him until the pain diminished enough for him to think about such things as upper body strength.

But he hadn't allowed for Nurse Early. She never handed his water cup to him; she always placed it on the table that pivoted in front of him. She wanted him to learn to feel for a glass without knocking it over.

Once, he became so frustrated that he knocked the glass across the room with a sweep of his right forearm. He heard the splat of water and the skip and bounce of the plastic cup with supreme satisfaction.

But Nurse Early came back every day. During the morning hours, she stretched his arms, working first for mobility, then strength, letting him use a half-pound dumbbell.

"Give me more weight," he demanded. He wanted to exercise like a man. Early wouldn't allow it, so he quit lifting her half-pounder.

Their running battle continued for weeks. Secretly, Ken liked the nurse's perfume. Just to know a woman was nearby, just to smell her scent—he liked that.

One day, feeling particularly lousy, Ken refused to attend occupational therapy. "I ain't no basket weaver!" he complained.

"Oh yeah?" said Early, and plopped him down hard in his wheelchair. "You are going to occupational therapy!" she said. "And I'll tell you what else you are going to do. You are going to act like a soldier. Your injuries don't entitle you to anything more than the United States Congress is willing to pay for. And it's not paying me to pity you!"

She kept up this harangue during the struggle of getting him belted into his chair and wheeling him out of the ward. She kicked the door open for emphasis. Then, she hung a fast right into a room that smelled of freshly washed towels and linen.

"We're in the laundry room, Ken," she said. "We're alone." Now her voice was calm, lower. "I want to tell you something."

You've told me enough already, he thought.

"I know you're hurting," she said, her voice warming with compassion. "I know that's why you don't want to do any of this. But you have to try. You have to try now while it still hurts. When the pain's gone, the opportunity's gone. You won't be able to regain any mobility if much more time passes. Ken, put all that stubbornness to use. I know you can do anything you put your mind to. From now on, it's just going to take a whole lot more effort. You're going to have to find your own way to do things. But you can. You will. If you were a quitter, you would be dead by now. I need you to show me the courage that kept you alive."

"Nurse Early?" said Ken.

"What?"

"What size do you want your stupid basket?"

"I'LL DO IT"

Ken's ward contained all the worst cases. He didn't need his eyes to know that. He was the only one among the half-dozen in the room who could scoot himself out of bed into a wheelchair. Still, he and his ward mates found ways to entertain themselves. On Friday nights, they called a fried chicken delivery service and ordered in buckets and beer.

One Friday afternoon they were kidding each other, feeling high, anticipating their big night of chicken and suds, when Dave Crowley suggested, "Hey, Ken, why don't you get us some

munchies? You can get in that chair now. Go on down to the PX
and buy out the store."

"Yeah, what else can we do with our money?" said another.

Ken had never been able to turn down a dare. "I'll do it," he said.

He was in his wheelchair and nearly past the nurse's station
when the nurse on duty called, "Where you going, Ken?"

"To the PX. Going to get my friends some munchies."

"That's good," she said absently, as if talking to a three-year-old
who said he was flying to the moon.

Ken kept rolling. He would show them all.

By the time he reached the end of the first hall, he was wondering how he would ever make it. He waited until he heard the
familiar scraping slide of a doctor's surgical booties.

"Can you tell me how to get to the PX, sir?" Ken asked.

"Turn left here, then down this corridor, a right at the next,
two more, another left, another right, and then you had better
ask again."

"Okay, thanks."

Powering his wheelchair with his left hand and scraping the
wall for guidance with his right, Ken worked his way past door-
jambs, heating ventilators, abandoned IV stands, and laundry carts.
Several steep ramps gave him more than a thrill, and he wondered
how he would ever wheel his chair up again on his way back.

He remembered instructions for one or two corridors at a time,
then asked again. Finally, he turned into an open space and
smelled hamburgers and fries. A few more hand-pumps, and he
hit a table and chair and knew he had arrived.

But how would he make his way along the cafeteria rail? How
would he know what was in front of him? He was swiveling his
head around, trying to take in as much as he could through his
useful senses, when he heard someone talking close by.

"Soldier?"

Was the person speaking to him?

"Soldier?"

"Yes, sir?"

"I'm Colonel McDermott. Are you supposed to be here?"

"I'm doing rehabilitation on the blind ward, sir. My buddies asked if I would go to the PX and get them some munchies. I'm the only one who can get in a chair, so I came down."

"That ward's up on level 9, isn't it?"

"Yes, sir."

"Level 9. That's a long way. Did somebody bring you down?"

"No, sir. I came down by myself."

"What's your name, soldier?"

"Specialist 4 Ken McGarity, sir. I was a door gunner with the Ghostriders."

"Would you like me to help you find your snacks?"

"Yes, sir. Appreciate it, sir. I was wondering how I was going to manage."

"You don't mind if I wheel you through the line, do you?"

"No, sir. It's a long way down from level 9."

As Colonel McDermott wheeled Ken past the candy bars, pretzels, and potato chips, the room grew quiet. So quiet that when the cash register chinged on Ken's purchases, it sounded like a symphonic *ta-da!*

"How are you going to get that bag up to level 9 with you, private?" the colonel asked.

"Easy." Ken tucked his change in the front pocket of his hospital gown, then grasped the top of the grocery bag between his teeth. He couldn't hold the bag in his lap because his leg stumps were too short to balance anything. He took a big breath through his nose, preparing to roll.

"Private McGarity?" said the colonel.

Ken let loose of the bag to answer. "Yes, sir?"

"I'm saluting you, private."

"Yes, sir."

Suddenly, the quiet was broken as applause rang out around him. "Carry on," said the colonel.

Outside the PX, Ken powered up the first ramp, a new energy in his hands and arms. He could do it. He had found his way down here; now all he had to do was find his way in life. Nurse Early had said he could do anything he put his mind to. Now, for the first time, he was sure that he could. He hadn't realized how tightly his doubts and fears had been gripping him, trying to suffocate the life that remained.

Relief teared in his eyes. He was truly going to make it!

HIS TOUGHEST CASE

Twenty years later, in 1989, Peter McPherson, a young freelance journalist, called Dr. Kenneth Swan, then a professor of surgery at the University of Medicine and Dentistry of New Jersey. McPherson was writing about trauma care, and Swan was an ideal candidate to interview. Besides his experience in Vietnam, he was chief of surgery for trauma care at his university hospital; he also remained in the army reserves as a full colonel.

"Dr. Swan, what was the toughest case of your career?" the young journalist asked. A twenty-year-old memory, long suppressed, rose to the surface of Swan's mind. It was the memory of a soldier wounded so badly that Swan's colleagues had thought him better off dead.

"What ever became of the guy?" asked McPherson after he heard the story.

"He made it back to the States," said Swan. "That's all I know."

When Peter McPherson's article appeared, dozens of readers wrote letters to the editor, wanting to know what had become of the young soldier. McPherson called Kenneth Swan and suggested that they find out. Neither was sure he would like what they might find.

Their search became almost an obsession that carried them through many dead ends and bureaucratic runarounds. But two years later, in July of 1991, Dr. Swan finally learned that his former patient, Kenneth McGarity, was now living in Columbus, Georgia; that he had a wife and two daughters, had completed his high school education, attended Auburn University, and had learned to scuba dive.

"You must have the wrong guy," Swan said to the person at the Veterans Administration. "My patient had brain damage. He was a double amputee. How would he ever learn to scuba dive?"

"Doctor, this is your patient. If you want to call him, go ahead."

When Swan placed the call, an upbeat Southern male voice answered. It was Ken McGarity.

Swan explained about Peter McPherson, the story, his search. "I would like to meet you," he concluded.

"Fine," said McGarity. "You can fill in a lot of holes for me, Dr. Swan. There are a lot of things I would like to know about that day."

So it was that on September 25, 1991, almost twenty-three years to the day since their fateful encounter in Pleiku, Dr. Swan and Ken McGarity met outside the McGarity home in Columbus, Georgia, accompanied by McPherson and a photographer. When McGarity extended his hand in greeting, Dr. Swan recognized his own work, the amputated right pinkie finger. In that instant, he felt a bond with this man. And in the long conversation that followed, he was able to offer Ken McGarity reassuring answers to a host of troubling concerns. Like survivor's guilt. Maybe he should have been left to die, as so many had suggested to him. Perhaps there had been someone who needed medical attention more.

"No, no," Swan reassured him. Treating Ken had not meant denying treatment to anyone else.

Then Dr. Swan raised his own troubling questions. Had it been worth it? Was Ken happy to be alive?

"I'll tell you something," Ken said to the doctor. "Being blind in a wheelchair has its problems, I won't deny that. But really, it's not so bad, Dr. Swan. I would be dead if it weren't for you!"[2]

FIGHT FOR THEM

Peter McPherson's story was published in the *Washington Post,* and soon ABC's *20/20,* the *New York Times, Good Housekeeping,* and even the *Times* of London came calling.

The mass media ate up the story on its most superficial terms— after twenty years, doctor finds worst-case patient living a full and happy life. What an inspirational tribute to the indomitable human spirit! But real life is always more complicated than it appears, and it certainly was for Ken McGarity. At the time of Dr. Swan's visit, Ken, his wife, Theresa, and their girls were living through the most difficult part of Ken's healing.

In 1989, two years before Dr. Swan met the McGaritys, Theresa had had a nervous breakdown and had been hospitalized. The two girls, Alicia and Elizabeth, had gone to live with Theresa's parents. When Theresa came out of the hospital, she knew she had to confront Ken about the problems that had been building since their marriage in 1971, problems that had contrib- uted to her own illness. To do so, she had to return to the place she had once considered her dream house—a place where Ken now lived alone, a sickened ghost of the man she had married.

When she crossed the threshold, the familiar scent and atmo- sphere hit her with the chilling effect of a mausoleum's dead air. She knew she couldn't bear to stay here for more than a few min- utes, but what she had learned in the hospital told her that she needed to do this, especially if she and Ken were going to have the slightest chance at a future.

"Theresa! Theresa!" Ken called, bumping his way out of the bedroom. "Theresa, you're back. Come here, and let me kiss you."

She bent down, but gave him only her cheek to kiss. Then she stepped away. "I'm not back, Ken. Not yet."

"They want to keep you longer at the hospital?"

"No. I'm getting better. But I'm not really going to be well until you get the help you need. And our marriage isn't going to work until you get the help you need."

"The help I need?"

"Ken," Theresa said, "you have post-traumatic stress disorder."

But Ken was so frightened of becoming a sedated zombie in a VA hospital that he drove Theresa out of the house rather than admit the truth. He knew he was addicted to Valium and alcohol, though neither delivered any relief from his anxieties. So he continued to live alone, desperate and despairing, haunting his back bedroom—his cave of refuge.

His fears went into a feedback loop: He didn't want to end up a zombie in a hospital, but if he sought help now, the doctors would put him exactly where he didn't want to be. He saw no way out, so he kept delaying, refusing to make a decision, refusing to take action.

He prayed, screaming out to God to rescue him. Once again, God answered. But this time, God declared clearly what was required of him.

You want your wife back? God asked. *You want your daughters back?*

"More than life itself," he told the Lord.

Then you're going to have to fight for them, Ken. You're going to have to get help.

THE HARDEST PART OF THE HEALING

Ken remembered how it all started. He hadn't become an addict and a recluse all at once, although he had known something was wrong almost from the moment he came home from the hospital.

He had lasted only ten days with his parents before he knew
he had to move out. He heard them whispering about him, talking past him, arranging what he would do and when. So he
announced he was getting his own place, and within a day he had
rented a one-bedroom apartment. His younger brother had been
a big help, bringing his friends around to visit and taking Ken
out joyriding, to the movies, to bars. Someone always wanted to
hear the war stories of a garrulous, hard-drinking vet.

His mother came over occasionally to cook for him. The rest
of the time Ken ate out of cans. He could survive on his own.
The only problem was, he couldn't sleep. Away from his buddies
and the booze, alone in his bedroom, the darkness closed in, like
a circling sniper. He heard every sound. The cars passing his
apartment building. Moths fluttering against the floodlight close
to his window. Worse, the occasional airplane passing overhead
sent him diving out of his wheelchair to the floor in sudden panic.

To save his sanity, he established a perimeter against the darkness. His bed was his bunker, and he kept his rifle beside him.
Sometimes he spent hours working its bolt action, the oiled mechanism precise and secure. Sometimes he hypnotized himself to
sleep that way. But the nightmares wouldn't stop.

After he met and married Theresa in 1971, he improved for
a time. She could not understand why he kept a gun by his side
at night. First she moved it out of the bed and set it beside the
nightstand. Then under the bed. Finally, she persuaded him to
put it in the closet.

Theresa's mother was a strong Christian, and at her encouragement, the newlyweds started attending church regularly. Married
life cut way down on Ken's time hanging out in the bars, as well as
his drinking at home with his buddies. Physically and emotionally,
he began to feel much better. He even slept, with only the occasional nightmare throwing him into Theresa's arms.

A year after their wedding, despite Ken's partial "shrapnel vasectomy," Theresa came home with the news that they were going to be parents. After Alicia's birth, holding his perfect newborn daughter in his arms, Ken experienced the deepest possible joy. Six years later, he felt the same as Elizabeth came into the world.

Bolstered by Theresa's love, his delight in his daughters, and his increased sense of security, Ken studied hard and passed a high school equivalency exam, then began taking classes at Auburn University. He learned how to scuba dive, trusting the instructor enough to hold his hand and go down into the waters. Nothing seemed impossible—as Nurse Early had told him, he only had to find his own way of doing things.

But after about ten years of marriage, Ken began to go downhill. His moods grew dark and irritable, punctuated by violent rages. His wife and daughters became afraid of him after he threw a few punches their way, and they moved out.

Despite the nightmare their life became, Theresa never abandoned Ken. After she came home from the hospital and first confronted him about his post-traumatic stress disorder, she kept coming back to the house periodically to check on whether he had changed his mind about therapy.

Finally, after a year of separation from his family, Ken broke. "I want you back, hon," he told her. "I want the kids back. I know this is what God wants me to do. I'm willing. But I just don't want to get help from the VA."

Theresa knew that he meant it; she could hear it in his voice. She had gone back to college herself, majoring in counseling, and with access to psychological treatment resources, she soon found a psychiatrist qualified to treat Ken as an outpatient.

"Why do you think you feel a need to have a safe area around you?" Ken's counselor asked. "To 'keep the perimeter clear,' as you say?"

They had arrived at this question only after two months of therapy sessions. Now Ken knew the answer.

"The day the B-40 hit me, my whole world exploded. I suppose I'm trying to keep that from happening again."

"Exactly."[3]

RUNNING TOWARD GOD

The publicity generated by Ken's meeting with Dr. Swan caused other vets to get in touch with him, to share their own war stories and their problems as civilians. Ken realized he was not alone in his struggles. Many others had suffered post-traumatic stress disorder.

He was especially pleased to hear from guys in his old Ghost-rider helicopter unit, like Otto Mertz, the soldier who had dragged him to safety in the midst of the firefight. As they renewed their friendship, Ken discovered that Otto was a strong Christian, and Ken spilled out the story of his prayer out by the lake and about waking up to find that it had happened—that God had taken his eyes and legs. He confessed that he had been running from God ever since, from God's sheer, terrifying power and the wrath of his judgment.

"Why does God seem to be wrathful?" Otto asked. "If you look at your life and see all the wonderful things you've got, don't you have to say that he's a loving God?"

Ken was brought up short. He had to acknowledge that God had given him a wonderful wife, two lovely daughters, and free-dom from financial worries. God had preserved his life and had been nurturing it all along, despite his many failings.

From that point on, Ken began to accept this loving God as the Lord of his life. He no longer wanted to run from God; he wanted to run toward him, into his embrace. While Ken had known God before, he was finally fully at peace with him.

How thankful Ken was that God, through Dr. Swan, had not left him to die that day at Pleiku.

*I see no reason for attributing
to man a significance different
in kind from that which belongs
to a baboon or a grain of sand.*

OLIVER WENDELL HOLMES

CHAPTER 8

WHATEVER HAPPENED TO HUMAN LIFE?

As you read, keep the following questions in mind:
- What denial is at the core of the "culture of death"?
- How does "a radical dualism between body and soul" account for the sexual liberation of recent generations?
- In what ways is abortion "about more than abortion"?
- If autonomy reigns, regard for what is lost? What does this mean in life-and-death matters?

Life is a miracle, a sacred gift from God. Nobody knows this better than Ken McGarity. Admittedly he did not live "happily ever after." Yet despite his pain and handicaps, Ken is thankful to be alive. He knows how precious life is.

What is the meaning of human existence? Why are we here? What is the value of human life? The most vexing cultural issues of our day—abortion, assisted suicide, euthanasia, genetic engineering—all turn on questions about what it means to be human, about the value of human life and how life should be protected. Which, in turn, center on the question of our origin.

Christians believe that God created human beings in his own image. And because human life bears this divine stamp, life is sacred, a gift from the Creator. He and he alone can set the

boundaries of when we live and when we die. Against this, as
we saw in earlier chapters, is the naturalistic belief that life arose
from the primordial sea through a chance collision of chemicals,
and that over billions of years of chance mutations, this biological
accident gave rise to the first humans. Millions of people today
accept this basic presupposition that we are little more than
grown-up germs—just as Dave and Katy saw at Epcot—which
logically leads to the conclusion that a person has no greater
significance than a baboon, as Oliver Wendell Holmes so bluntly
put it.

These two worldviews are antithetical, and this antithesis lies
at the very heart of our present cultural crisis. The question of
where life comes from is not some academic argument for scientists to debate. Our understanding of the origin of life is intensely
personal. It determines what we believe about human identity,
what we value, and what we believe is our very reason for living. It
determines who lives and who dies. This is why ethical questions
surrounding human life have become the great defining debate of
our age.

The Christian's commitment to life cannot be dismissed as
some "love affair with the fetus," as critics have charged, or as a
desire to impose a repressive Victorian morality.[1] Instead, the
Christian is driven by a conviction, based on biblical revelation,
about the nature of human origins and the value of human life.
That's why, confronted with a mangled soldier clinging to life,
Dr. Kenneth Swan did not consult some ethics book or debate
abstract principles. Having been brought up in a culture steeped
in the Judeo-Christian tradition that human life has intrinsic value
because it was made in the image and likeness of God, he simply
did what came naturally. He saved the man's life.

But what was once a culture of life is today being overtaken by
what John Paul II calls a "culture of death," a naturalistic ethic
sweeping across the entire spectrum, from the unborn to the old

and infirm, from the deformed and disabled to the weak and defenseless. Relentlessly pursuing its own logic, <u>this culture of death denies that the human species is superior to all other biological species, and it ends by threatening life at every stage.</u> It has advanced so far that assisted suicide (euthanasia) is now a protected constitutional right in one state, paid for by the state's Medicaid program, and infanticide is being openly advocated by respected professors and scientists, with hardly a ripple of public shock or dissent.

Surely this is hyperbole, you may say. Alarmist rhetoric. Well, let's take a look at how the most fundamental convictions upon which Western civilization has rested for two millennia are being replaced by a naturalistic ethic of pragmatism and utilitarianism.

CULTURAL PARADIGM SHIFT

The shift from a culture of life to a culture of death has been like a shift in the tectonic plates underlying the continents—as sudden as an earthquake, when measured against the long view of history. It occurred largely in the 1960s, although as with so much else in American life, the fault lines were evident centuries earlier, in the Age of Reason and the Enlightenment.

The Human Mind as Fixed Point

The beginning point might be fixed in the seventeenth century, when French mathematician René Descartes resolved to doubt everything that could possibly be doubted. After intense inner questioning, Descartes concluded that he could doubt everything except the fact that he doubted, everything except his mental experience. This conclusion led to his famous statement: "I think, therefore I am." With this, Descartes unleashed the revolutionary idea that the human mind, not God, is the source of certainty;

human experience is the fixed point around which everything else revolves.[2]

Ironically, Descartes was a sincere Christian, a devout Catholic, to the end of his life. But there is nothing Christian about his philosophy. By establishing the human mind as the judge of all truth, his philosophy eventually rendered God irrelevant. And since traditional notions of morality and social order are largely derived from Christianity, these moral conventions likewise crumble when God is dismissed as irrelevant or nonexistent.

The Death of God

The death of God means the death of morality. This logic was pressed by a decidedly odd prophet—Friedrich Nietzsche, a German who peered into the soul of our century and later went insane. "Whither is God?" Nietzsche asked in 1889. "I will tell you, *we have killed him*—you and I. All of us are his murderers!"[3] He was incensed that the majority of Westerners had not yet fathomed the devastating consequences of the death of God. He wanted them to understand that if they gave up belief in God, they must also give up biblical ideas of morality and meaning.

It's My Body, Isn't It?

This is exactly what the twentieth century has done. If we were not created by God—and therefore are not bound by his laws—if we are simply the most advanced of the primates, why shouldn't we do whatever we choose? In the 1960s, the Age of Aquarius, such views exploded into popular consciousness, aided by inhibition-freeing drugs. Sexual liberation would be the means to create a new, open, egalitarian society where "nobody can tell us what to do with our bodies." As Christian apologist Peter Kreeft says in his brilliant satire "The World's Last Night," we have a society today in which the "one intrinsic good, self-justifying end, self-evident value, meaning of life, and non-negotiable absolute is sex."[4]

Radical Dualism

What makes this view possible, notes Professor Robert George of Princeton, is a radical dualism between body and soul, a dualism that can also be traced back to <u>Descartes, who reduced the body to little more than a machine operated by the mind.</u> It follows that the body is not really "me," but something separate from my real self—an instrument to be used, like a car or a computer, for whatever purposes I choose. Therefore, what I do with my body, whether I use it for physical pleasure or even discard it if it becomes inconvenient, has no moral significance.

Carried to its logical conclusion, this view implies that sexual acts between unmarried people or partners of the same sex or even complete strangers have no moral significance. Since the body is reduced to the status of a mere instrument of the conscious self, it can be used for any form of pleasure and mutual gratification as long as there is no coercion.[5] Even disposing of physical life is of no greater moral consequence than discarding an old set of ill-fitting clothes.

This logic is what caused the Supreme Court to decide in *Roe v. Wade* (1973) that a human fetus is not a person and can therefore legitimately be destroyed.[6] Justice Harry Blackmun, who wrote the majority opinion, acknowledged at the time that if a fetus were a person, then its right to life would be guaranteed under the Fourteenth Amendment (which instructs the states that they may not deprive "any person of life, liberty, or property"). In order to uphold the right to abortion, the Court had to argue that though the fetus is biologically human, it is not a legal person. What's more, if the justices acknowledged that the fetus changed from a nonperson to a person at any stage of pregnancy, then abortion would become an unlawful deprivation of life—in short, murder. The Court ruled that the fetus is a nonperson with no rights at all at any stage of pregnancy. Only the mother is a person, with a "right to privacy."

"Choice" as Value

Roe v. Wade was the leading edge of a powerful social movement, fueled by sexual politics, to free the individual from the yoke of allegedly repressive moral restraints. "Choice" over what to do with one's own body became the defining value of the 1970s and 1980s—all the while ignoring the fact that choice in itself cannot possibly be a value and that value depends on *what* is chosen.

A CULTURE OF DEATH

Abortion has always been about more than abortion. It is the wedge used to split open the historic Western commitment to the dignity of human life. In 1973, when pro-life proponents warned that *Roe* was taking us down a slippery slope to all manner of horrors, they were mocked as alarmists. Later events proved them prescient.

From Abortion to Infanticide

With the "Baby Doe" case in 1982, in Bloomington, Indiana, the relentless demand for choice crossed the great divide—from the living fetus in the womb to the living baby outside the womb—and America moved from abortion to infanticide. Baby Doe was born with a deformed esophagus, making it impossible for him to digest food. Doctors proposed a fairly simple operation, a procedure that had proven to be 90 percent successful. But the parents refused to grant permission for the operation, even though they knew this meant certain death for their newborn infant. Their own doctor concurred. The reason? Infant Doe was also born with Down's syndrome.[7]

Two Indiana courts declined to intervene, and six days later Baby Doe had starved to death. Columnist George Will, who himself has a Down's syndrome child, declared flatly, "The baby was killed because it was retarded."

In the flurry of controversy over Baby Doe, something shocking came to light: Handicapped infants were quite routinely being allowed to die. As early as 1975, a poll of pediatric surgeons revealed that 77 percent favored withholding food and treatment in the case of defective babies. And in an Oklahoma hospital it was discovered that the pediatric staff weighed "quality of life" in deciding whether to treat handicapped children or let them die. Among their considerations of "quality" were race and family income.[8]

Abortion as "Positive" Health Policy

Even earlier, of course, the philosophical groundwork for eliminating defective babies was being laid by the abortion debate. In the 1960s, the American Medical Association (AMA) had passed a resolution endorsing abortion when "an infant [may be] born with incapacitating physical deformity or mental deficiency."[9] Several states had also already passed laws allowing abortion in such cases. When such a law was passed in New York, a commentator at WCBS radio hailed it, saying, "Abortion . . . is one sensible method of dealing with such problems as over-population, illegitimacy, and possible birth defects."[10]

The first public official to declare abortion a positive public health policy was Arkansas State Health Director Joycelyn Elders, later surgeon general of the United States. Abortion, she said, has "an important and positive public health effect," reducing "the number of children afflicted with severe defects."[11] Abortion was no longer treated as a wrenching tragedy, a decision reached with agonizing reluctance. Instead, it was a positive good—a means for improving the species.

To support her position, Elders cited a study showing that the number of Down's syndrome children born in Washington State in 1976 was "sixty-four percent lower than it would have been without legal abortion."[12] What Elders did not say is that most people with Down's syndrome are only moderately retarded and grow into adults who are capable of holding a job and living independently. And if the birth parents cannot cope, there is a waiting list of couples eager to adopt these children. Yet today, they are being targeted for elimination.

Because people with Down's syndrome have an extra chromosome, the condition can be diagnosed before birth by amniocentesis. Insurance companies readily agree to pay for these tests; often, if the test is positive, the insurance companies also cover abortion. But the same companies will not pay the $100,000 or more that is required to sustain the first year of the baby's life. How many couples facing such a choice can withstand the economic pressure? Not many. Studies show that 90 percent choose abortion—often under pressure from doctors.[13]

For any "unwanted" or "defective" baby who may manage to slip through this front line of defense, there is always the ultimate solution. Francis Crick, who along with James Watson won the Nobel prize for the discovery of the double helix structure in DNA, advocates that all newborns be screened to determine who should live. All who fail to reach a certain level on the Apgar test, used to determine the health of newborns, would be euthanized.[14]

Ramifications of Evolutionary Psychology

Steven Pinker of MIT, who has replaced the late Carl Sagan as the nation's great science popularizer, is injecting these views into the mainstream. He is central casting's perfect choice for the job: glib and genial, just professorial enough to carry authority but friendly enough not to be threatening. Pinker is the most prominent proponent of evolutionary psychology, the latest version of sociobiology, which reduces living things to products of their genes.

The reason evolution has produced the human mind, Pinker claims, is merely to protect the genes and "maximize the number

of copies of the genes that created it." Applying these concepts to
the issue of infanticide, Pinker argues that the newborn is basically
a gene carrier and that before bonding with their newborn children, parents have always "coolly assessed" the "biological value
of a child (the chance that it will live to produce grandchildren),"
based on its health and the parents' own resources. When mothers
kill their own newborns, Pinker said, we must "understand" their
actions, remembering that "the emotional circuitry of mothers has
evolved" by natural selection to include "a capacity for neonati-
cide" in cases where the mother feels she lacks the resources to
raise the child. In short, while denying that he supports the practice, Pinker suggests that infanticide is built into our "biological
design," and we cannot blame people for doing it.[15]

Rationale? Dualism

The rationale for all of this is, again, a dualism between body
and person. Rights belong only to persons, so if someone can
be reduced to a nonperson, then he or she has no rights. Peter
Singer, newly appointed Ira DeCamp Professor of Bioethics at
Princeton, openly advocates permitting parents to kill disabled
babies on the basis that they are "nonpersons" until they are rational and self-conscious. As nonpersons, he says, they are "replace-
able," like chickens or other livestock. And Singer does not stop
there. He goes on to advocate killing incompetent persons of any
age if their families decide their lives are "not worth living."[16]
(This is the unspeakably inhumane brand of ethics that students
in some of our nation's most prestigious schools are now learning.
And what will happen when these elite students move into positions of power?)

The baby in the womb, having been reduced to the status of a
nonperson, is then demonized in pro-choice literature as a hostile
aggressor against the mother, and abortion is dressed up as self-
defense. Northeastern University professor Eileen McDonagh

claims that the fetus "massively intrudes on a woman's body and expropriates her liberty," justifying the "use of deadly force to stop it," analogous to cases of rape, kidnapping, or slavery.[17]

The Cherished Right

Clearly, anyone who threatens our cherished right to do whatever we please with our bodies must be stopped, by whatever means necessary. Arguing that the fetus is a violent and dangerous intruder, and justifying the use of deadly force to repel it, are the functional equivalent of having Susan Smith justify the drowning of her children with the defense that they were interfering with her freedom to be with her new lover.

If the Body Is Merely an Instrument . . .

And yet many well-meaning Americans, including Christians, have bought into the "choice" argument. They don't see that abortion, infanticide, and euthanasia are all part of the same package. The logic that supports abortion as a "useful social policy" to prevent the birth of "defectives" or to reduce welfare and crime, applies with equal force at all stages of life. If the body is merely an instrument of the self, if it has no inherent dignity, then we are free to dispose of it at will—or others are free to dispose of it for us.

The abortion lobby understands very well that all these issues are interconnected, which is why feminist organizations fight relentlessly to defend even partial-birth abortion—a gruesome, barbaric procedure that the AMA has denounced and that even its practitioners have acknowledged is not medically necessary. This is also why the abortion lobby fights so furiously against any diminution of abortion rights—even minor limits such as parental notification. A school must obtain a parent's consent before giving a child an aspirin, but the abortion lobby fights tooth and nail against any statute requiring parental consent for abortion.

Why do pro-choicers oppose even modest limits? Because they understand that abortion represents a worldview conflict: God and the sanctity of life versus the individual's moral autonomy. They can give no quarter.

Autonomy Reigns?

But once the principle of autonomy and choice is established, there is no way to maintain any higher value for life. A few years ago, a former inmate whom I had discipled, and who had then gone on to become a gifted young pastor, took his own life. I was shattered when I received the news. In addition to grief, I blamed myself. I should have seen it coming, should have done something.

A friend, seeing my distress, sought to comfort me. "Don't blame yourself, Chuck," she said, gently gripping my arm, "and don't judge. It was, after all, *his* life."

His life. *His* choice! The well-intentioned remark drove me deeper into despair, because this middle-aged woman was reflecting the beliefs of a majority of Americans.

In the Name of Compassion

Opinion polls show consistent and growing public support for euthanasia—in the name of patients' rights and compassion, of course. In fact, one of the organizations aggressively promoting euthanasia is named Compassion in Dying. Even Dr. Kevorkian, who put his "patients" to death ignominiously in cheap trailers or motel rooms and then dumped the bodies at local hospitals, evaded prosecution again and again before finally being convicted and imprisoned.

In 1997, Oregon became the first state to legalize assisted suicide, enacted by public referendum. So far, challenges to the law have been successfully rebuffed. In the states of Washington and New York, referenda were passed barring the practice, but

challenges to both were successfully sustained in lower courts. To
grasp the connection between abortion and euthanasia, one need
only look at the way these lower courts argued in favor of assisted
suicide.

Liberty Reinterpreted

The judges in both cases relied on a 1992 decision, *Planned
Parenthood v. Casey*. In this decision, the Supreme Court, while
upholding modest state restrictions on abortion, attempted to
place the alleged constitutional right to abortion created by *Roe
v. Wade* on a more secure legal footing. Its dictum defined liberty
as the right to make "intimate and personal choices . . . central to
personal dignity and autonomy. . . . [It] is the right to define one's
own concept of existence, of meaning, of the universe, and of the
mystery of human life."[18]

In the Washington assisted-suicide case, Federal District Judge
Barbara Rothstein echoed *Casey's* definition of liberty. After all,
what could be more "intimate and personal" than the choice
of whether to live or die? Hence Rothstein argued that assisted
suicide "constitutes a choice central to personal dignity and autonomy."[19] The Ninth Circuit Court of Appeals sustained her.
(Although the Supreme Court eventually set this decision aside,
it offered largely pragmatic reasons for not permitting assisted
suicide at this time.)[20]

The Right to Kill

The Ninth Circuit Court decision sustaining Rothstein was written by Judge Reinhardt, a liberal activist, who, in his 109-page
opinion, included a chilling footnote: In cases where patients are
unable to give informed consent, a surrogate may be appointed to
act for them in consenting to assisted suicide.[21] With a stroke of
the pen, the court crossed the divide—from suicide to euthanasia,
from voluntary death to involuntary death. This represented the

first time a U.S. court has ever endorsed the private use of lethal force (outside the context of abortion), a move that undercuts the very essence of the American social contract in which individuals agree to renounce the use of lethal force in return for the state's preserving order. As moral theologian Russell Hittinger says, this is no longer the right to die; it's the right of some Americans to kill other Americans.[22]

The line between assisted suicide and euthanasia has become a legal fiction. Legislatures or courts may slow the process here or there, but the train is out of the station and roaring down the tracks. And even if euthanasia is not yet secure as a constitutional right (except in Oregon), its practice is on the increase.

Without a Biblical View . . .

We must be clear, however, that the Christian is not morally obligated to save life by all measures and at all costs. Many Christians believe that it is morally acceptable to withdraw life support when the technology is merely sustaining life artificially. Many also believe that it is morally acceptable to refuse extreme intervention or heroic measures to resuscitate a patient who is beyond recovery. But without a biblical view of human life, the distinction between refusing heroic measures and actually helping to hasten death can quickly become blurred.

"We're Not Dead Yet"

In the end, these issues all hinge on the way a culture views human life. If human life bears the stamp of the divine Maker, it is infinitely precious. But if human life is simply a product of biology or nature, a utilitarian unit, then utilitarian values become the dominant determinant. Get the dying, the infirm, the disabled, the nonproductive out of the way of the living.

When two assisted-suicide cases were being heard in the U.S. Supreme Court, protesters gathered on the front steps of the

building. Most of them were disabled Americans, many in wheel-
chairs, and many carried signs that proclaimed "We're Not Dead
Yet." These protesters know that if the Court legalizes physician-
assisted suicide, it will create tremendous pressure on the handicapped to take that option and stop being a burden on society.
Looking at life through the eyes of a quadriplegic who requires
vast sums of money and human resources for support, or through
the eyes of a Ken McGarity, we see with laser-beam focus the
deadly logic of a worldview that degrades life.[23]

The supremely tragic irony in all of this is that a supposedly
exalted view of human reason has led to such a degraded view of
human life. When Descartes declared, "I think, therefore I am,"
he had no idea his slogan would lead to a culture in which what
I am is determined by what *other* people think.

BRAVE NEW BABIES

Descartes also did not anticipate where this degraded view of
human life would lead us.

Aldous Huxley's prophetic novel *Brave New World* opens with
a visit to a laboratory where rack upon rack of glass bottles clatter
across conveyor belts. Each bottle contains a carefully fertilized
human egg immersed in amniotic gel, predestined for a specific
purpose, ranging from the alphas (the intellectuals) to the gammas
(the manual laborers). Defects are eliminated, and most females
are neutered.

In the story, this remarkable process creates an ideal species
capable of living in complete harmony and stability, a species free
of all antiquated encumbrances such as family and child rearing.
To ensure the unfettered pursuit of happiness, free sex is encour-
aged, and an all-purpose drug called Soma is readily available. Life
is perpetual bliss. When it becomes burdensome or inconvenient,
it is gently and mercifully ended.

Selective Breeding

Huxley's vision was not some bizarre fantasy. He was expanding on ideas then being soberly discussed among his friends in the intelligentsia. Eugenics—the idea of improving the human race through selective breeding—did not originate in Hitler's laboratories. It originated in the 1920s and 1930s among respectable and sophisticated men and women in places like London, Philadelphia, and New York.

On the horizon of today's brave new world looms the specter of genetic engineering, the ultimate attempt to create a race free of defects. Hardly any obstacles remain in the path of this final expression of human autonomy. In March 1997, when Dolly, the first cloned sheep, was introduced to the world, scientists and doctors hailed the experiment as the dawn of a new era, promising great medical and commercial benefits. At a hastily called hearing in the United States Senate, scientists assured the legislative body that no one would attempt to clone human beings. Everyone nodded . . . until one brash, outspokenly liberal senator shocked those gathered by asking the logical question: "Why not?"

Why Not?

Why not indeed? If life is simply the result of a chance naturalistic process—molecules colliding and combining in a primordial soup—why shouldn't we control our own genes or create new life forms? We are simply adapting a natural process to its most advantageous use.

Achieving *Brave New World* technology is only a matter of time. Research called EG—for extracorporeal gestation—is now under way at the Juntendo University in Tokyo and Temple University in Philadelphia and is intended to create an artificial womb for severely premature babies.[24] If the research is successful, the same technology will surely be developed further, until the artificial womb can house a fertilized egg. There is almost no stopping the technological imperative: If something *can* be done, it *will* be done. Then, with the role of biological parents rendered superfluous, humanity can take another important step along the road to total autonomy.

Truly our capabilities have exceeded our ethical and moral grasp.

Pandora's Box

Though most Christian ethicists support assisted reproduction if used only to help restore natural function, the problem comes when we do things never done in nature—for example, genetic combinations impossible in nature. The technology of in vitro or in vivo fertilization also makes possible a host of morally dubious practices, such as the harvesting of fetal tissue for medical purposes, the disposal of fertilized eggs that are capable of becoming fetuses, and surrogate parenthood, which has already opened a Pandora's box. We hear of a woman who is impregnated by her son-in-law and gives birth to her daughter's child. A female Episcopal priest has the sperm from three men mixed (so she will not know who the father is), is impregnated, and gives birth. Gays and lesbians mingle at gatherings they call "Sperm-Egg Mixers," where they examine one another with an eye toward selecting good genes. Two lesbians may contract with a gay man for his sperm for artificial insemination, or two men may contract with a lesbian whom they chose to be a surrogate mother.[25]

There is little left in our culture to restrain or even slow the process.[26] In Britain, a prestigious committee under the leadership of Dame Mary Warnock, professor of moral philosophy at Cambridge, was organized to provide moral guidance on these questions. But Dame Warnock herself says that in these issues "everyone has a right to judge for himself." And who could possibly object?

Something within Us Stirs

The answer, of course, is anyone who is truly human. Even in Huxley's *Brave New World,* the great dramatic moment comes when the protagonist, appropriately called "the savage," who was born the old-fashioned way, escapes the world of endless pleasures in pursuit of his natural parents.

Something within us stirs ceaselessly in search of meaning and purpose and connection. Christians know this something as the soul, or the *imago Dei*—the image of God within us. Because of the doctrine of creation, we know life has worth. We know it is rooted in something beyond the test tube or colliding atoms, even as many voices around us say otherwise.

DISCUSSION QUESTIONS

CHAPTER 7

1   Put yourself in surgeon Swan's place. If a commanding officer "grilled you" for devoting the "full resources of the hospital" to saving this life, under these circumstances, how would you respond?

2   Trace the ups and downs of Ken McGarity's emotional journey. At each stage, describe the specific role of Ken's "supporting cast."

3   From Ken's story, what do you learn about the value and role of community?

4   In what ways can you as individuals and as a group encourage people who are in some way living "on the edge"?

5 At the end of this story, Ken is "thankful." For what does Ken's story make you thankful?

CHAPTER 8

6 Read Psalm 139:1-18. Do you think David, writer of this psalm, would have said, "I think, therefore I am"? Why or why not? Think in terms of a biblical worldview. What word(s) might replace Descartes' "think"?

7 What do you see in Psalm 139 that counters what you've read about:

a. mind-body dualism?

b. the "culture of death"?

8 Modern teens and adults often resort to the line "It's *my* body, isn't it?" On what biblical grounds could you take issue with them? (See 1 Cor. 3:16; 1 Cor. 6:15-17, 20.) On what pragmatic grounds could you disagree with them?

9 In what ways is abortion about more than abortion? In what ways is "choice" about more than choice?

10 What significance do you see in the slogan We're Not Dead
Yet?

11 Read Jeremiah 1:5-8. What does this passage say to you?
What does it embolden you to do?

ROLE PLAY
Refer to the directions for role play, at the end of session 1
(pp. 27–28).

CONVERSATION STARTER
Two people are sitting in a coffee shop, one with a Christian
worldview and one who believes that "autonomy reigns." Role-
play a conversation in which one person starts by saying, "When
it comes to abortion and when-to-die issues, I think it's all up to
individual choice. When I've had enough, I just want to 'check
out' of here."

CLOSING SUMMARY
What is the most important point you want to remember from
this session?
    Consider sharing this with the group.

LIFE WORTH LIVING

*It is not natural to see man as a
natural product, it is not seeing
straight to see him as an animal.
It is not sane. It sins against the
light, against the broad daylight
of proportion, which is the principle
of all reality.* G. K. CHESTERTON

CHAPTER 9

IN WHOSE IMAGE?

As you read, keep the following questions in mind
- In what ways does the biblical worldview create a sustainable, rational, and liberating basis for human life?
- How does the Christian worldview provide hope for the future?
- How does the Christian worldview motivate us to serve others?

Can anyone really live with a completely naturalistic view of human life, that human beings are just primates? Some people in Denmark thought so.

In 1996, the Copenhagen Zoo announced a new exhibit. In a glass-walled cage in the primate house, a pair of *Homo sapiens* would be on display. Since people can observe *Homo sapiens* just about anywhere, at any time, the exhibit seemed a strange choice. But zookeeper Peter Vestergaard had a specific agenda. The exhibit, he said, would force people to "confront their origins," causing them to "accept" that "we are all primates." After all, he added, humans and apes share 98.5 percent of the same chromosomes.[1]

Yet what an amazing difference that 1.5 percent seems to make. While their hairy neighbors were busy staring at the ceiling, swinging from bars, and picking lice from each other's pelts, the caged *Homo sapiens*—otherwise known as Henrik Lehmann and Malene Botoft—read books, worked on a motorcycle, checked E-mail on the computer, sent and received faxes, and, when necessary, adjusted the air conditioning. The *Homo sapiens* were also free to leave their cage whenever they encountered the primitive urge for a movie, a candlelight dinner, or a night at the opera. Unlike their animal neighbors, the humans on display refused to heed the call of nature in public, and when Lehmann was asked whether he and his female partner would display "intimate behavior" in front of the spectators, he sniffed, "That's not interesting."[2]

A few weeks later the exhibit was terminated, and both *Homo sapiens* departed the monkey house. Were they any the wiser for their experience? One would hope so. I suspect they were forced to recognize that they were qualitatively different from the apes in the surrounding cages.

The short-lived experiment certainly made a point—though not the one the zookeeper intended. Naturalistic philosophy holds unwaveringly to the proposition that we are descended from ape-like creatures, making us primates in the highest stage—at least so far—of the evolutionary process. Yet the test of any worldview is whether it conforms to reality, to the way things really are. And the reality is that humans are fundamentally different from animals. The truth is *in* us, put there by the divine stamp of the Maker, and as hard as we may want to, we cannot dislodge it. In fact, every attempt to deny the truth about our nature is doomed.

SUSTAINABLE, RATIONAL, AND LIBERATING BASIS FOR LIFE

Only the Judeo-Christian view of life conforms to reality, to the nature and character of the human condition as we actually experience it. Only the biblical view creates a sustainable and rational and truly liberating basis for human life. This becomes abundantly clear when we examine Christianity and naturalism from several perspectives: compatibility with the scientific evidence, human dignity, the ultimate meaning in life, our destiny, and service to others.

Compatibility with Scientific Evidence

Which worldview corresponds with the scientific evidence? Respect for human life at all stages is supported by growing scientific data showing that even before birth, the fetus is fully human. Sonogram pictures show the unborn child clearly responding to stimuli; and due to advances in neonatology, doctors now consider the baby in the womb a real patient. Medicine is performing diagnostic and therapeutic wonders on unborn babies, including surgery. The growth of scientific knowledge "is causing us to regard the unborn baby as a real person long before birth," says Mike Samuels in *American Family Physician*.[3] The pro-life position is supported by empirical, rational arguments that are accessible to everyone.

Robert George of Princeton University has pressed these arguments among the nation's leading scholars, including well-known deconstructionist Stanley Fish of Duke University. In 1998, George was invited to debate Fish at a meeting of the American Political Science Association: The debate would be about the nature of the evidence for and against abortion. In earlier writings, Fish had dismissed arguments against abortion as based on "religious conviction" alone, while suggesting that the case for abortion is based on "scientific facts." George's position held that, on the contrary, the arguments against abortion are based on scientific data that a fetus is indeed human.

George sent his paper to Fish in advance, and then the two joined two hundred other scholars who had gathered for the debate. But the event was cut short at the start when Fish rose, threw his own paper on the table, and announced, "Professor George is right, and he is right to correct me. Today the scientific evidence favors the pro-life position."

The audience sat in stunned silence.[4]

Basis for Human Dignity

Which worldview provides the strongest basis for human dignity? Scripture tells us that "God created man in his own image, . . . male and female he created them" (Gen. 1:27). This is a breathtaking assertion. Humans actually reflect the character of the ultimate Source of the universe. How could anyone even theoretically conceive of any more secure basis for human dignity?

The Christian worldview also tells us that humans have an eternal destiny, which likewise bolsters human dignity. Throughout history, most cultures have had a low view of the individual, subordinating the individual to the interests of the tribe or state. And if Christianity were not true, this would be quite reasonable. "If individuals live only seventy years," said C. S. Lewis, "then a state, or a nation, or a civilization, which may last for a thousand years, is more important than an individual. But if Christianity is true, then the individual is not only more important but incomparably more important, for he is everlasting and the life of a state or a civilization, compared with his, is only a moment."[5] This explains why Christianity has always provided not only a vigorous defense of human rights but also the sturdiest bulwark against tyranny.

And because we all stand on equal ground before God, Christianity gives a sound basis for social and political equality. Each individual stands directly accountable before the Creator, writes Abraham Kuyper; there are no intermediaries, no spiritual hierarchies between us and God. It follows, then, that we "have no claim whatsoever to lord [it] over one another, and that we stand as equals before God, and among men." Consequently, the

Christian worldview "condemns not merely all open slavery and systems of caste, but also all covert slavery of women and of the poor."[6]

Multiculturalists insist that all cultures are morally equivalent.[7] But this argument blurs over genuine differences. For in a culture that truly upholds the God-given dignity of individuals, widows are not burned on their husband's funeral pyre (as they are in India), people are not sold into slavery (as they are in the Sudan and elsewhere), and life is not sacrificed to satisfy ancestors or an angry god (as still happens in some primitive cultures). No, for all of the faults of its adherents—and there have been many—Christianity has accorded men and women dignity unlike any other belief system in the world.

Since the Enlightenment, secular thinkers in the West have sought to ground human rights in human nature alone, apart from biblical revelation. The French Revolution was fueled by rhetoric about the "rights of man." Yet without a foundation in the Christian teaching of creation, there is no way to say what human nature is. Who defines it? Who says how it ought to be treated? As a result, life is valued only as much as those in power choose to value it. Small wonder that the French Revolution, with its slogan "Neither God nor master," quickly led to tyranny and the guillotine.

When the thirty-nine misguided members of the Heaven's Gate cult took their lives, broadcasting magnate Ted Turner dismissed the tragedy with the cynical comment: "It's a good way to get rid of a few nuts. There's too many people anyway."[8] His comments succinctly, if callously, sum up the beliefs of growing numbers of Americans who have succumbed to the notion that there is nothing special about human life, that we are all simply part of nature.

In that naturalistic worldview it is only logical to place the goal of population control above the dignity of human life and to resort to any means available to reduce the human population in order to preserve Mother Nature from being depleted and despoiled. From this perspective, humans are often seen as aggressors against a pristine nature. Of course, Christians believe we are responsible to protect God's creation, to be good stewards, and to exercise dominion. But naturalists go far beyond responsible environmentalism to outright reverence. In the movie *The River*, an all-American farm family sits around the dinner table, and the young children recite the blessing, which turns out to be a prayer to nature: "Thank you earth, thank you sun, we are grateful for what you have done. Amen."[9]

The same logic drives the animal rights movement, as it denigrates human life in its efforts to make the human species equal with all others. These attempts often turn nasty, with animal rights activists throwing paint on women wearing furs; nasty and destructive, strapping explosives around tree trunks to blow up loggers and save the spotted owls; nasty, destructive, and sometimes silly, raiding restaurants to liberate lobsters.

When animal rights proponents discover the inherent irrationality of their own belief system, as they sometimes do, this debased view of human life can produce a kind of schizophrenia. Such is the case when two trendy causes collide. Animal rights groups like PETA (People for the Ethical Treatment of Animals), popular among Hollywood stars, militantly oppose animal research, to the point of sometimes raiding and vandalizing laboratories and kidnapping laboratory animals.[10] But animal research, which was essential in developing the polio vaccine and hosts of other lifesaving breakthroughs, is also crucial to AIDS research, another favored cause in Hollywood. So AIDS activists now find themselves eagerly supporting animal research, even while their political allies smash laboratories.[11]

The naturalistic view of human life is simply not rationally sustainable, yet the cultural elites cling to it with slavish devotion.

Some years ago, an editorial in *California Medicine* stated that the traditional Judeo-Christian ethic "is being eroded at its core and may eventually be abandoned." The anonymous editorialist welcomed the shift from a "sanctity of life" ethic to a "quality of life" ethic, arguing that "it will become necessary and acceptable to place relative rather than absolute values on such things as human lives, the use of scarce resources, and the various elements which are to make up the quality of life or of living which is to be sought."[12]

It's hard to imagine anything more terrifying than living in a culture where human life is made relative to lesser values, such as material resources. The principle we see at work here is that any culture that kills God inevitably ends up worshiping some other deity—and will gladly sacrifice even life itself in the service of this new deity.

Ultimate Meaning in Life

Which worldview gives a sense of meaning and purpose? One of the arguments often used for abortion is that children should not be brought into a world where they are destined to suffer poverty or abuse. Likewise, a common argument for euthanasia is that the gravely ill have no purpose for living. These views seem persuasive only because the purpose of life has been reduced to something woefully shallow, a simplistic sense of happiness as emotional fulfillment, career success, or wealth. Many modern Americans have lost any sense of a higher destiny. Their lives have no aim or goal.

It is as if a friend were to suggest that you load your family in the van and start out on a trip. No destination in mind, no time constraints, no limit to your choice of recreation. "Take as long as you wish, and return whenever you choose," your friend urges. "It's all yours. You're free. Go."

"You're crazy," you say. "Why would I want to take my family on some aimless journey?"

Yet that is exactly what modern humans are told to do in today's world: make our lives into aimless journeys; follow our whims and impulses. To be sure, the voices of the culture dress it up a bit. They celebrate the joys of autonomy, our right to create our lives and even our selves, our endless choices and conveniences, our freedom from all the quaint conventions and legalisms of a less enlightened era. Whether it be the chatter of the elite, the steady torrent of TV, or the politicians' babble, we constantly hear that personal choice is the only thing that will produce "happiness"—the most sacred goal of American life. We are cast free, only to drift helplessly, like someone embarking on a journey with no destination and no answer to the oldest philosophical question of all: What is the purpose of life?

I've seen examples of this in many places. My wife and I live in an area of Florida that, a few years ago, began attracting upscale retirees: presidents of auto companies, comptrollers of major corporations, and high-powered barons of Wall Street, who settle into their luxurious gated communities, surrounded by manicured golf courses, fine restaurants, and swaying palms. They enjoy the American dream come true: no worries, no work, and golf every day.

Many of them follow a predictable pattern. Like a man I'll call Charlie. Freed from the pressures of work, Charlie eagerly trots off to the golf course every morning, ends up on the nineteenth hole for a few relaxing drinks, and then arrives home in time to scan the *Wall Street Journal* and take a short nap. At five o'clock Charlie gets out his chartreuse sports jacket with matching checked pants, part of a new wardrobe he purchased at a local, pricey men's shop. No more navy pinstripes for Charlie. Then it's off to the club for a cocktail party thrown by his neighbors. (We'll call them the Hewitts.)

Different neighbors host the party each night, either at their home or at the club. After six weeks or so, the cycle comes back to the Hewitts, and around they go again.

After a cycle or two, Charlie begins to detect a certain sameness to the conversation. People grumble about taxes, share tidbits about the new neighbors, complain about the yard people or the plumber, compare their grand edifices . . . and, of course, comment on the weather.

"It's a good one today, eh, Charlie?"

"Oh yeah, but getting muggy."

Charlie even finds his enthusiasm for golf waning somewhat, which is strange because he's loved golf all his life. And he finds that when he skims the *Wall Street Journal,* he sometimes experiences a wave of nostalgia for the good old days when he *had* to read it—and when it often quoted him. He misses striding into the office every morning to begin a new day.

It's usually only six months, a year at the most, before the disillusionment sets in. Charlie is no longer interested in talking about books or current events; the banal cocktail chatter has hollowed out his brain. Besides, he's drinking too much, and his memory is slipping. He's short-tempered and easily angered, particularly by incompetent plumbers and yard people. When someone swings a car door open recklessly and dings his new Mercedes, he gets really depressed. He begins to wonder how many golf games he has left before he dies. In fact, thoughts like that begin to wake him up in the middle of the night.

Sadly, I know a lot of Charlies—once vital, productive people who have deteriorated into heavy-drinking bores. They long for a sense of fulfillment and dignity that no amount of pleasure can provide.[13]

The fact is, men and women cannot live without purpose. The *Westminster Shorter Catechism* asks:

"What is the chief end of man?

"To glorify God and enjoy Him forever."

It's a staggering thought that we can know and glorify and enjoy the sovereign God, fulfilling his purpose through our lives. This all-consuming purpose gives life meaning and direction in all circumstances.

This explains why quadriplegic Joni Eareckson Tada can live so joyfully even though she is confined to a wheelchair. Like Ken McGarity, she has known great pain and suffering and distress; but she also knows she has a purpose, and her work with handicapped people has touched the lives of millions. I've been with Joni many times and have never seen her anything but cheerful and bent on encouraging others. She is far more fulfilled than many people who are in robust health or surrounded by material abundance.

Pleasure, freedom, happiness, prosperity—none of these is ultimately fulfilling because none can answer that ultimate question of purpose. What is the purpose of human life? <u>Knowing that we are fulfilling God's purpose is the only thing that really gives rest to the restless human heart.</u>

Assurance about Ultimate Destiny

Which worldview provides a sense of assurance about our ultimate destiny? Every view of human life is shaped by two great assumptions: our origin and our destiny—where we came from and where we are going. The latter asks, Is this life all there is? Is death the end of all our deepest aspirations and longings?

The existentialists pointed out that if there is nothing beyond the grave, then death makes a mockery of everything we have lived for; death reduces human projects and dreams to a temporary diversion, with no ultimate significance. But if our souls survive beyond the grave, as the Bible teaches, then this life is invested with profound meaning. Everything we do here has a significance for all eternity. The life of each person, whether in the womb or out, whether healthy or infirm, takes on an enormous dignity.

This is why death has always been surrounded by rituals and religious rites, for it is death that reminds us of our own mortality and forces us to ask disturbing questions about the meaning of our own life. I recall how this struck me in April 1994 at the funeral of Richard Milhous Nixon, thirty-seventh president of the United States, a man whose career profoundly defined my own life before my Christian conversion. Even after Watergate and my own prison term, I visited him often, for the truth is, I admired Nixon. He was a decent and caring man, at heart a true son of his Quaker mother, with an idealist's passion for peace. More important, he was a friend. For me, the funeral was especially poignant and painful.

For three days, thousands of visitors, oblivious to the cold rain, surrounded the Nixon Library in Yorba Linda, California, filing past the coffin in silent tribute. On the afternoon of the funeral service, the area was cordoned off for blocks around, as limousines brought in the great and near great from every continent. The library parking lot had been turned into an open-air sanctuary, with fifteen hundred chairs arranged in rows, marked off strictly according to protocol. Present were four former presidents and the incumbent president, cabinet members and presidential staff, diplomats and foreign dignitaries, and most members of the Congress of the United States.

As military pallbearers marched the coffin bearing the body of Richard Nixon to its resting place, the crowd fell silent and stared somberly at the proceedings, the silence broken only by the roar of jets overhead.

It had rained that morning, but as the crowd waited, evanescent shafts of light filtered earthward through the dark clouds. Minutes passed. The stillness became eerie. I looked around and saw that everyone was simply staring at the coffin. All the power in the world sitting there, mesmerized by a coffin—forced in those moments to come face-to-face with the one reality about which all their power could do nothing: their own mortality. It was a vivid picture of the great human quandary.

Then, standing before that audience, with millions more watching on television, Billy Graham preached one of the greatest and most timely messages that I have ever heard him preach. He preached about Christian hope, a hope that no other world belief system offers.

For the secularist, death is like stepping off a cliff into a black abyss of nothingness. The Muslim faces a fearsome judgment, and for many Eastern religions, the prospect is equally grim: After death, the law of karma decrees that people must pay the penalty for what they have done in this life, being reincarnated according to their past deeds. But for the Christian, assured of eternity with the Lord, "to die is gain" (Phil. 1:21).

Motive for Service and Care

Which view of life provides the most certain motive for service and care of others? This is a crucial question, for any society in which citizens care only for themselves cannot long endure. Such a group cannot even be called a society. Rather, it is a collection of self-centered individuals, destined to implode when their selfish pressures reach a certain point, which is exactly what we are moving toward in our own self-absorbed culture.

Scripture commands believers to love our neighbors as ourselves (Matt. 19:19), to care for widows and orphans (James 1:27), to be a Good Samaritan (Luke 10:30-37), to feed the hungry, clothe the naked, visit the sick and imprisoned (Matt. 25:36). But where does this compassion, this compulsion to care for others, come from?

The answer is that if we know we are created by God, then we should live in a state of continuous gratitude to God. Gratitude, said G. K. Chesterton, is the mother of all virtues. Gratitude for every breath we breathe, every moment we have to enjoy the wonders of his creation and all that is ours—family, work, recreation. Gratitude that the Son of God took away our sins and paid our debt on the cross. Compelled by this gratitude, we desire to love him and live as he commands. "This is love for God: to obey his commands" (1 John 5:3).

People often ask me why I've continued to work with prisoners for more than twenty-five years, to go back to prison, to frequent places rampant with disease, violence, and massive depression. My answer is simple: Out of gratitude for what Christ did for me, I can do nothing less.

Obedience to Christ's commands changes our habits and disposition. That's why, through the centuries, so many of the great humanitarian causes have been led by Christians, from abolishing the slave trade to establishing hospitals and schools. At one point in the early nineteenth century in America, there were more than eleven hundred Christian societies working for social justice. Today, two of the world's largest private organizations caring for the hungry are Christian agencies: Catholic Relief Services and World Vision. And the Salvation Army alone does more for the homeless and destitute in most areas than all secular agencies combined.

To be sure, well-meaning secularists can show compassion, give generously to charities, and offer help to the downtrodden and the needy. As creatures made in the image of God, all human beings practice some of the virtues. But the critical question is, What motivates them? As sociobiologists have so persuasively argued, if humans are a product of natural selection, then even the most caring acts are performed, ultimately, because they advance our own genetic interests. Kindness is a disguised form of selfishness. What this means is that even the most conscientious secularists have no rational basis for being compassionate; they act on solely subjective motives—which could change at any given moment.

Of course, Christians often fail to follow their own convictions. But when believers are selfish, they are acting contrary to their own beliefs. By contrast, when secularists are compassionate, they are acting contrary to the internal logic of their own worldview.

There is also no basis for compassion in alternative worldviews like Eastern pantheism. While visiting a prison in Trivandrum, India, some years ago, I saw firsthand what the Hindu caste system does to human dignity. Our team was welcomed warmly to the old colonial-era structure by a group of well-dressed corrections officials, and we were immediately surrounded by a cordon of Indian guards in summer dress khaki uniforms: knee-length shorts, red epaulets on their shoulders, and swagger sticks tucked under their arms. As they marched us toward the flower-bedecked center platform, I could almost hear the strains of the "Colonel Bogey March."

In the field before us were at least a thousand inmates, most of them "untouchables." Their sweaty, dark skin contrasted with their white loincloths, their only clothing. They rested submissively on their haunches, their eyes fearfully darting from side to side. These men were not only condemned to this horrid institution, where they were caged in squalid holes with no toilets or running water, but even worse, they were totally dehumanized, treated as outcasts. No Hindu who lived by his own beliefs could care one whit for them.

I spoke that day through a Hindi translator, sharing my own testimony and the gospel of Jesus Christ. When I talked about forgiveness for sins, I saw many eyes open wide, startled. This was a radical thought. In Hinduism there is no forgiveness. Whatever wrong one has done in this life must be repaid in one's next incarnation according to the iron law of karma. As a result, no consistent Hindu would practice charity, for that would interfere with the law of karma.

A new life in Christ? Their sins washed away? Freedom? The

inmates were astounded by these ideas. A thousand pairs of eyes riveted on me intently, many of them glistening with tears.

After the prayer of invitation, I startled the guards and dignitaries by jumping down off the platform and walking toward the crowd, thrusting out my hand to the first man I could reach. It was pure impulse; I sensed that I should let the men know that I wanted to touch them.

Suddenly, like a flight of birds, men rose to their feet and circled around me. For the next twenty minutes, I shook every hand I could. Most of the men just reached out and touched; I felt hands all over my arms and chest and back. They were desperate to "touch," to know that the love God offers is real. They kept swapping positions with one another, until virtually all had made some kind of physical contact with me.

Later, these men went back to their grim cells. No one can say how many of them submitted to Christ that night, but at least one message got through—that in Christianity they are not untouchable.

The Christian worldview compels us, in a way no other worldview can, to genuinely care for one another.

REAL HOPE

The high view of human life offered by Christianity is not a veneration of mere biological life. The Christian understands that our real hope is in the spiritual realm, so that some things are more important than biological life. Obedience to God is one of those things. Like a scarlet thread, such obedience winds its way from the lions' den to the cross to Chinese house churches to services held underneath trees in the barren regions of southern Sudan. Justice and truth are values far dearer than biological life.

The naturalistic view of life pervades every area of Western culture, but nowhere with greater effect than among young people.

At every turn, they are bombarded with hedonistic, self-gratifying messages. Day in and day out, they are bombarded with the message that life is all about toys and pleasures and satisfying every hormonal urge.

Yet deep within each of us is a truth that cannot be suppressed, even under such a relentless assault. It is in our very nature, the way we are created, no matter how hard we may try to suppress it. And it bursts out in the most unlikely places—even at a presidential press conference.

In 1993, Bill Clinton boldly seized an opportunity to identify with the young people of our country by holding a question-and-answer session on the MTV network with a group of high school students. The show is best remembered as the occasion when students asked the president whether he wore boxer shorts or briefs. But not all the questions were so trivial.

Near the end of the session, an eighteen-year-old from Bethesda, Maryland, raised her hand. "Mr. President," said Dahlia Schweitzer, "it seems to me that singer Kurt Cobain's recent suicide exemplified the emptiness that many in our generation feel. How do you propose to . . . teach our youth how important life is?"

Clinton's answer was what one would expect from a skilled politician and a child of the sixties. He told her that young people need improved self-esteem; they need to feel that "they're the most important person in the world to somebody."

But Kurt Cobain *was* important to somebody—to lots of somebodies. He was a star. Yet he still felt the "emptiness" that young Dahlia was talking about; nothing in his personal worldview could teach him "how important life is."

In reporting the exchange between Dahlia Schweitzer and the president, the *New York Times* commented, tongue in cheek, that the president did not seem to have a legislative answer to the question.[14] Well, we should be grateful for small things, I suppose.

One can only imagine some politician proposing a "meaning of life" bill.

Obviously, the question is not something that can be addressed by political measures or by our culture's dominant worldviews. As the existentialist philosopher Albert Camus argued, if God is dead, then "there is [only] one truly serious philosophical problem, and that is suicide. Judging whether life is or is not worth living amounts to answering the fundamental question of philosophy."[15]

Yet Augustine offered an answer that is as true today as it was sixteen hundred years ago: "You made us for yourself, and our hearts find no peace until they rest in you."[16] Only when we find God can we halt this restless search, because the very essence of our nature is the *imago Dei*—the image of God—implanted in us by the Creator.

Why have we dealt at such length with creation and the question of origins? Because the most important implication of creation is that it gives us our basic understanding of who we are; our view of origins determines our view of human nature. The dignity of human life is not only a burning issue of our day, it is intensely personal to me.

I know all the theological arguments and believe I can hold my own in any rational debate. But when all is said and done, I find the ultimate answer to the question of life in the smiling face of my grandson Max.

CHAPTER 10

GOD MAKES NO MISTAKES

As you read, keep the following question in mind:
- What does the story of Max say to you?

Max is a handsome eight-year-old with dancing blue eyes and a shock of blondish hair that tosses about as he bounces up and down in his favorite spot in our home—my office chair. "Grandpa's chair, Grandpa's chair," he squeals with delight, his face breaking into a broad smile.

Max and I see each other a lot, and our times together are, to put it mildly, intense. Sometimes we go to a super McDonald's, the ones with the playland of slides and brightly colored boxes of plastic balls. No matter how many children are sliding and jumping among the balls, Max is always having the best time. If the other kids leave, he will continue jumping up and down, chanting, "More kids, more kids."

Everybody notices Max. Not only because he is so adorable, but because he is different. He is set apart by his sometimes moody, impenetrable stares, his failure to respond.

You see, Max is autistic.

Max arrived by way of a frightening and difficult delivery requiring an emergency cesarean section. So there was special joy in the Colson family when our daughter, Emily, came through the

surgery and Max arrived safely, appearing to be a robust and
healthy baby boy. But soon we noticed that Max was not behaving
as expected. He was colicky and irritable. He would scream loudly,
and he seemed especially bothered by unfamiliar noises. He didn't
crawl when he should have and was late walking. Then there were
the distant stares and the periods of withdrawal. We denied what
was becoming evident for as long as we could, confidently assuring
each other that he would grow out of it.

I confess that I prayed hard for some miraculous intervention.
I also asked the tough questions. How could God let this happen
to my beloved daughter's only child? *It isn't fair,* I told God many
times. And at first I found it difficult to enjoy Max as much as I
did our other grandchildren. I couldn't bounce him on my knee
or get him to look at me. Often he would scream when I picked
him up.

But as he got a little older, we noticed something else. Max has
a special capacity for love.

Patty and I usually ask our grandchildren to accompany us
when we make our annual delivery of Angel Tree gifts at Christmas. So when Max was only two, he was with us as we headed
out into the country to visit a family who lived an hour from our
home. As we drove, Emily and Patty and I talked about the two
little girls we were going to see. Their father was in prison, and
their mother was away working, so they were living with their
grandparents. We vowed that when we got there, we would try as
hard as we could to let these two girls know how much they were
loved. All the while, Max sat in his car seat, sucking his thumb,
his expression fixed in the distant, unconnected stare characteristic
of his condition.

The grandparents were waiting in front of their home, a large
trailer set back on a wooded lot. As we walked through the front
door, Max, usually painfully shy with strangers, suddenly pulled
free of Emily's hand and ran across the living room straight for

the two little girls. He awkwardly embraced the younger one, a cute four-year-old with long blond pigtails, and then held his cheek against hers, smiling. He did the same thing with her six-year-old sister. Then, still smiling, he retreated to his mother's side.

Max had never done anything like this before. My only explanation is that he understood what we were talking about in the car—and he was determined to deliver the love for us.

One of the many great paradoxical truths of the Christian life is that the greatest adversity often produces the greatest blessings. I've certainly discovered in my own life the truth of James 1:2: "Consider it pure joy, my brothers, whenever you face trials of many kinds." And I've seen the truth of it in my daughter's life. Max was one of the stresses, we now surmise, that led to Emily's ending up as a single parent. But if she was discouraged by all this, she never showed it. And Max has changed my daughter from a lovely young girl into a mature Christian woman who sees her son as a gift from God.

On Max's sixth birthday, Emily wrote me a touching letter. "God created Max exactly the way he intended Max to be," she wrote. "Max was not a mistake in the way he was made. God had a definite purpose when he created Max as he did. I do not presume to know what God had or has in mind for his purpose, and I may never know all the intricacies of God's purpose for Max. What I do know is that Max is perfect in the way God created him."

Max hears things differently from other people, sees things differently, tastes things differently, and enjoys life differently. Yet his "joyous spirit and exuberance for life" are a great gift. "I've learned to look past the disability and see the individual," Emily wrote, "and now Max has become my greatest blessing."

Max is a blessing to others as well. "Max has an ability to affect people's lives more than anyone else I know," Emily continued.

"When Max enters a room full of people, it's like dropping a spoon into a blender—everyone stops and reacts. Just when people's lives are running along smoothly, everything blending as it should, in comes Max, this sweet, energetic, beautiful child who doesn't fit into their recipe. Everyone reacts in some way, good or bad. But eventually they become aware of their own actions and feelings, and this profoundly affects them. It is a wonderful experience for me to see someone who has not felt comfortable with Max take the chance and reach out to him."

Emily summed up her experience with these words: "God knew when he created Max that he would need extra help in this world, so God keeps his hands cupped around Max. He doesn't let him go. I know that wherever Max is, God is holding him gently in his hands. How could a child who is held by God be anything but a gift?"

The fact is that Max has touched more lives than any other little guy I know. Yet Max is exactly the kind of child that the modern eugenics crowd would snuff out in the womb—or, if his "defect" couldn't be detected there, then on the delivery table. Or even, if Francis Crick had his way, in the first weeks of life.

The dreadful truth is that the culture of death has taken a firm grip on the minds and hearts of otherwise responsible people in every walk of life. But when it comes to Max, these people are going to have to deal with my daughter first—and with me. Christians need to form a frontline defense for the Maxes of this world.

■   ■   ■

The real problem with this world is not deformity in the body; it's deformity in the soul. In a word, it's sin. Anyone who harbors an idealistic urge to improve the human race ought to look not to eugenics but to means for healing the sinful heart.

Yet the very notion of sin is unpalatable to the modern mind.

As a result, many of the brightest Western thinkers have con-structed a great myth to avoid facing the truth about sin and guilt. And ironically, this myth, more than anything else, has brought unimaginable havoc and misery into this century.

DISCUSSION QUESTIONS

CHAPTER 9

1 Read aloud Genesis 1:26-28, along with Genesis 2, which elaborates details of the creation of human life. Discuss the significance for us, the bearers of the image of God, that God is

spiritual

rational

moral

social

aesthetic ("good")

creative

active

2 In this Genesis account, what mandates did God give human beings?

3 How did the mandates given to Adam and Eve require them to use every aspect of their image-bearing potential? (Review the attributes of that image, outlined in question 1.)

4 On what basis does the biblical worldview uphold the dignity of individuals, men and women alike? Why is this so important in this day and age?

5 According to the *Westminster Shorter Catechism,* what is the "chief end" of humanity? Why is it difficult to firmly grasp this important issue? Discuss this as it relates to various seasons of life: adolescence, young adult years, midlife, and retirement.

6 Compare the Christian hope of eternal life with the after-death scenarios provided by other belief systems. What significance does this have for you here and now, on "this side" of eternity?

7 "When believers are selfish, they are acting contrary to their own beliefs. By contrast, when secularists are compassionate, they are acting contrary to the internal logic of their own worldview." Discuss this in terms of your own experience.

8 Refer again to the seven God-image attributes in question 1. How are you using these attributes to the glory of God?

9 In what ways would your community benefit if all the Christians living in it lived fully as God's image-bearers?

10 The *Book of Common Prayer* includes this prayer: "For the good earth which God has given us, and for the wisdom and will to conserve it, let us pray to the Lord. *Lord, have mercy.*" What would living out this prayer mean for you this week?

CHAPTER 10

11 How does the story of Max help us to see that every life is worth living when it is recognized as having been made in the image of God?

12 Read Psalm 139:13-18. Does this refer to all people? What does this say about God?

13 Brainstorm about ways you can minister to the disabled (like Max) and their parents (like Emily) in your community.

ROLE PLAY

Refer to the directions for role play, at the end of session 1
(pp. 27–28).

CONVERSATION STARTER

Ingrid Newkirk from People for the Ethical Treatment of
Animals has claimed that "a rat is a pig is a dog is a boy," the
implication being that we are "just animals." Assume someone
said this to you. Drawing on all you've learned in this book,
engage in a conversation with this naturalist.

CLOSING SUMMARY

What is the most important point you want to remember from
this session?

Consider sharing this with the group.

WHAT'S AHEAD

This book is just the first in the three-part Developing a Christian Worldview series that addresses overarching worldview issues. We recommend that you continue your study with book 2: *The Problem of Evil*. In six sessions this book addresses the second and third worldview questions: What has gone wrong with the world? and What can we do to fix it? This book explores not only the deep questions about sin, evil, and suffering but also how various worldviews attempt to fix the problem with their offers of salvation. Again, these worldview questions and answers are foundational to our experience as Christians, and the related discussions will help you identify and confront the many worldviews that promise redemption through false saviors.

Book 3, *The Christian in Today's Culture*, in six sessions covers a fourth significant question: So how, now, shall we live out our Christian worldview? This book gives examples of countless Christians who are putting feet to their faith and transforming their families, schools, and neighborhoods as well as the arenas of economics, law and politics, science, the arts, music, and popular culture. This call to action and the related discussions will inspire you and equip you to become part of God's redeeming force in this new millennium.

NOTES

INTRODUCTION

1. Read the story of my conversion in *Born Again* (Old Tappan, N.J.: Chosen, 1976).
2. Abraham Kuyper, *Christianity: A Total World and Life System* (Marlborough, N.H.: Plymouth Rock Foundation, 1996), 39–40.
3. Ibid., 41.
4. Cornelius Plantinga Jr., "Fashions and Folly: Sin and Character in the 90s," (presented at the January Lecture Series, Calvin Theological Seminary, Grand Rapids, Michigan, January 15, 1993), 14–15.
5. Ibid.
6. Ibid.
7. Richard M. Weaver, *Ideas Have Consequences* (Chicago: University of Chicago Press, 1984).
8. Samuel Huntington, "The Clash of Civilizations," *Journal of Foreign Affairs* (summer 1993): 22. Huntington identified the major power blocs as the Western, Islamic, Chinese, Hindu, Orthodox, Japanese, and possibly African regions.
9. James Kurth, "The Real Clash of Civilization," *Washington Times,* 4 October 1994.
10. Jacques Toubon, cited in "Living with America," *Calgary Herald,* 6 October 1993.

CHAPTER 1
DAVE AND KATY'S METAPHYSICAL ADVENTURE

1. Dave and Katy Mulholland are characters we created for this book, but their story is based on real events. The exhibits at Disney World and Epcot Center are described accurately, based on a visit in 1997. In a sense, Dave is Everyman, and Katy is Everyman's Teenager.

CHAPTER 2
SHATTERING THE GRID

1. The following discussion owes much to Norman Geisler's book *Cosmos: Carl Sagan's Religion for the Scientific Mind* (Dallas: Quest, 1983).
2. Carl Sagan, *Cosmos* (New York: Random, 1980), 4.
3. Carl Sagan, *Broca's Brain* (New York: Random, 1979), 282.
4. Ibid., 287.
5. Sagan, *Cosmos*, 242.
6. Ibid., 5.
7. Ibid., 243.
8. Ibid.
9. Ibid., 345.
10. Sagan, *Broca's Brain*, 271–75.
11. Carl Sagan was one of the scientists who formed the SETI Institute (Search for Extra-Terrestrial Intelligence). Sagan wrote the novel *Contact*, on which the movie *Contact* was based.
12. Sagan, *Broca's Brain*, 275.
13. Stan and Jan Berenstain, *The Berenstain Bears' Nature Guide* (New York: Random, 1984), 11.
14. Ibid., 10.

CHAPTER 3
LET'S START AT THE VERY BEGINNING

1. Ludwig Büchner, as quoted in Gordon H. Clark, *The Philosophy of Science and Belief in God* (Nutley, N.J.: Craig Press, 1964), 50.
2. Lincoln Kinnear Barnett, *The Universe and Dr. Einstein* (New York: William Morrow, 1968), 114 (emphasis in the original).
3. Paul C. Davies, *The Edge of Infinity: Where the Universe Came From and How It Will End* (New York: Simon & Schuster, 1982), 169.
4. Arthur Eddington, as quoted in Hugh Ross, "Astronomical Evidences for a Personal, Transcendent God," in *The Creation Hypothesis*, ed. J. P. Moreland (Downers Grove, Ill.: InterVarsity Press, 1994), 145–46.
5. Robert Jastrow, *Until the Sun Dies* (New York: Norton, 1977), 51.
6. Carl Sagan, *Cosmos* (New York: Random, 1980), 259.
7. The energy described here is energy available for work, not total energy.
8. William Lane Craig and Quentin Smith, *Theism, Atheism, and Big Bang Cosmology* (New York: Oxford University Press, 1993), 135.

9. M. A. Corey, *God and the New Cosmology: The Anthropic Design Argument* (Lanham, Md.: Rowman & Littlefield, 1993), 105.

10. Paul C. Davies, *The Accidental Universe* (Cambridge: Cambridge University Press, 1982), 90.

11. Heinz Pagels, "A Cozy Cosmology," *The Sciences* (March/April 1985): 38. See also Nancy R. Pearcey, "A Universe Built for Us: The Anthropic Principle," *Bible-Science Newsletter* (October 1990): 7; "The Anthropic Principle: The Closest Atheists Can Get to God," *Bible-Science Newsletter* (November 1990): 7.

12. George Wald, as quoted in Dietrick E. Thomsen, "A Knowing Universe Seeking to Be Known," *Science News* (February 19, 1983): 124.

13. Freeman Dyson, as quoted in Martin Gardner, "Intelligent Design and Phillip Johnson," *Skeptical Inquirer* (November 21, 1997): 17.

14. George Greenstein, *The Symbiotic Universe: Life and Mind in the Cosmos* (New York: William Morrow, 1988), 197.

15. Patrick Glynn, "The Atheistic Assumptions of Modern Society Are Being Challenged by the New Science," *National Review* 48, no. 8 (May 6, 1996): 32. See also Patrick Glynn, *The Evidence: The Reconciliation of Faith and Reason in a Postsecular World* (Rocklin, Calif.: Prima, 1997).

16. William A. Dembski, *The Design Inference: Eliminating Chance through Small Probabilities* (Cambridge: Cambridge University Press, 1998), chapter 2.

CHAPTER 4
LIFE IN A TEST TUBE?

1. *The Land Before Time* video series, Universal Pictures (1988).

2. The following discussion draws heavily from Charles B. Thaxton, Walter L. Bradley, and Roger L. Olsen, *The Mystery of Life's Origin: Reassessing Current Theories* (Dallas: Lewis & Stanley, 1992). See also Stephen C. Meyer, "Explanatory Power of Design," in *Mere Creation: Science, Faith, and Intelligent Design,* ed. William A. Dembski (Downers Grove, Ill.: Inter-Varsity Press, 1998), 113.

3. Stanley L. Miller, *From the Primitive Atmosphere to the Prebiotic Soup to the Pre-RNA World* (Washington, D.C.: National Aeronautics and Space Administration, 1996).

4. Fred Hoyle, *The Intelligent Universe* (New York: Holt, Rinehart, and Winston, 1983), 11.
5. Dean H. Kenyon and Gary Steinman, *Biochemical Predestination* (New York: McGraw-Hill, 1969).
6. From an interview quoted in Nancy R. Pearcey and Charles B. Thaxton, *The Soul of Science: Christian Faith and Natural Philosophy* (Wheaton, Ill.: Crossway, 1994), 230.
7. See Michael J. Behe, *Darwin's Black Box: The Biochemical Challenge to Evolution* (New York: Free Press, 1996), 210–16.
8. Arthur Fisher, "New Search for Life in Space," *Popular Science* 225 (October 1984): 44.
9. *Reunion in France,* MGM (1942).
10. See Thaxton, *The Mystery of Life's Origin;* Pearcey and Thaxton, *The Soul of Science;* and Stephen C. Meyer, "The Origin of Life and the Death of Materialism," *Intercollegiate Review* 31, no. 2 (spring 1996).
11. Richard Dawkins, *The Blind Watchmaker: Why the Evidence of Evolution Reveals a Universe without Design* (New York: Norton, 1996), 150.
12. Stuart A. Kauffman, *At Home in the Universe: The Search for Laws of Self-Organization and Complexity* (London: Penguin, 1996), 74.
13. Nancy R. Pearcey, "DNA: The Message in the Molecule," *First Things,* no. 64 (June/July 1996): 14.

CHAPTER 5
DARWIN IN THE DOCK

1. Douglas Futuyma, *Evolutionary Biology* (Sunderland, Mass.: Sinauer, 1986), 3.
2. "NABT Unveils New Statement on Teaching Evolution," *The American Biology Teacher* 68, no. 1 (January 1996): 61. The NABT statement created such an uproar that the organization subsequently dropped the words "unsupervised" and "impersonal." The change was largely cosmetic, however, since the remaining words "unpredictable" and "natural" were understood to mean essentially the same thing.
3. In technical language, Darwinism assumes that microevolution (minor change) is the engine for macroevolution (major transitions). This section draws on Nancy R. Pearcey, "Everybody Can Know: The Most Powerful Evidence Against Evolution," *Bible-Science Newsletter* (June 1987): 7.

4. Charles Darwin, *The Origin of Species* (New York: Penguin, 1958), 41–47.

5. Rick Weiss, "Mutant Moniker: A Tale of Freaky Flies and Gonzo Genetics," *Science News* 139, no. 2 (January 12, 1991): 30; and Dan L. Lindsley and Georgianna Zimm, "The Hard Life of a Mutant Fruit Fly," *Harper's Magazine* 284, no. 1703 (April 1992): 24.

6. Darwin's depiction of evolution as resulting from the gradual accumulation of countless infinitesimally minute variations demands that the fossil record preserve an unbroken chain of transitional forms from one species into another. But that is not the overall pattern that emerges from the fossil record. Instead, major groups of organisms appear in the fossil record suddenly, fully formed, without transitional forms leading up to them. See Jeffrey H. Schwartz, *Sudden Origins: Fossils, Genes, and the Emergence of Species* (New York: Wiley & Sons, 1999), 3.

7. Phillip E. Johnson, *Reason in the Balance: The Case against Naturalism in Science, Law, and Education* (Downers Grove, Ill.: InterVarsity Press, 1995). See also Nancy R. Pearcey, "Naturalism on Trial," *First Things*, no. 60 (February 1996): 64.

8. Jerry A. Coyne, "Not Black and White," *Nature* 396 (November 5, 1998): 35–36; Jonathan Wells, "Second Thoughts about Peppered Moths," http://www.trueorigin.org/pepmoth1.htm.

9. Luther Burbank, as quoted in Norman Macbeth, *Darwin Retried* (New York: Delta, 1971), 36.

10. Michael J. Behe, *Darwin's Black Box: The Biochemical Challenge to Evolution* (New York: Touchstone, 1996), 40–48. The functional integration of parts is a classic argument against Darwinism; it was first developed in the nineteenth century by George Cuirer. See Michael Denton, *Evolution: A Theory in Crisis* (Bethesda, Md.: Adler and Adler, 1985). See also Nancy R. Pearcey, "The Biochemical Challenge to Evolution," *Books & Culture* (November/ December 1996): 10.

11. Charles Darwin, *The Origin of Species*, (New York: New York University Press, 1988), 154.

12. Behe, *Darwin's Black Box*, 18–21, 36–39.

CHAPTER 6
DARWIN'S DANGEROUS IDEA

1. Stephen Gould, as quoted in Phillip E. Johnson, *Reason in the Balance: The Case against Naturalism in Science, Law, and Education*

(Downers Grove, Ill.: InterVarsity Press, 1995), 31. See also Stephen J. Gould, *Rocks of Ages: Science and Religion in the Fullness of Life* (New York: Ballantine, 1999).

2. William B. Provine and Phillip E. Johnson, "Darwinism: Science or Naturalistic Philosophy?" (videotape of debate held at Stanford University, April 30, 1994). Available from Access Research Network, P.O. Box 38069, Colorado Springs, CO 80937-8069, phone: (888) 259-7102.

3. Johnson, *Reason in the Balance*, 46–47.

4. Calvin Coolidge, as quoted in *The Journal*, (a Summit Ministries newsletter), 7.

5. Richard Rorty, "Trotsky and the Wild Orchids," *Wild Orchids and Trotsky: Message from American Universities*, ed. Mark Edmundson (New York: Viking, 1993), 38.

6. Richard Rorty, "Untruth and Consequences," *New Republic* (July 31, 1995): 27.

7. Richard Rorty, as quoted in Roger Lundin, *The Culture of Interpretation: Christian Faith and the Postmodern World* (Grand Rapids: Eerdmans, 1993), 15.

8. Richard Dawkins, *The Blind Watchmaker: Why the Evidence of Evolution Reveals a Universe without Design* (New York: Norton, 1987), 6.

9. The following discussion of Darwin and his contemporaries is based on Nancy R. Pearcey, "You Guys Lost," in *Mere Creation: Science, Faith, and Intelligent Design*, ed. William A. Dembski (Downers Grove, Ill.: InterVarsity Press, 1998): 73.

10. Nora Barlow, ed., *The Autobiography of Charles Darwin 1809–1882 with Original Omissions Restored* (New York: Norton, 1958), 87.

11. Ibid.

12. William Darwin, as quoted in John Durant, "Darwinism and Divinity: A Century of Debate," in *Darwinism and Divinity: Essays on Evolution and Religious Belief*, ed. John Durant (New York: Basil Blackwell, 1985), 18.

13. Francis Darwin, ed., *Life and Letters of Charles Darwin*, vol. 2 (New York: D. Appleton, 1899), 155.

14. David Duncan, *Life and Letters of Herbert Spencer*, vol. 2 (New York: D. Appleton, 1908), 319.

15. Leonard Huxley, *Life and Letters of Thomas Henry Huxley*, vol. 1 (New York: Macmillan, 1903), 246.

16. Thomas Henry Huxley, "Science and Religion," *The Builder* 17 (1859): 35.

17. Charles Hodge, *What Is Darwinism? And Other Writings on Science and Religion*, ed. Mark A. Noll and David N. Livingstone (Grand Rapids: Baker, 1994), 85, 155.
18. Richard Lewontin, "Billions and Billions of Demons," *New York Review of Books* (January 9, 1997): 31.
19. Ibid.
20. William Steig, *Yellow & Pink* (New York: Farrar, Straus & Giroux, 1984).
21. Carl Sagan, "In the Valley of the Shadow," *Parade* (March 10, 1996): 18.

CHAPTER 7
A MATTER OF LIFE

1. This story is based not only on interviews with Ken and Theresa McGarity as well as with Dr. Kenneth Swan, but also on information found in the following sources: Peter MacPherson, "The War Surgeon's Dilemma: Confronting His Vietnam Past: Was the Life He Saved Worth Living?" *Washington Post*, 7 January 1992; Colonel Kenneth G. Swan, MC USAR, "Triage: The Path Revisited," *Military Medicine* 161 (August 1996): 448–52; "Doubt Gone, Doctor Glad He Saved GI," *Chicago Tribune*, 28 November 1991; Joan Sanchez, "Army Doctor Tracks Down His Patient," *Los Angeles Times*, 8 December 1991.
2. Dr. Kenneth Swan stayed in touch with Ken McGarity, and soon after their first meeting, Swan called with extraordinary news. He had arranged for McGarity to receive the medals he had never been awarded because of a mix-up in record keeping. On January 30, 1992, at Fort Benning, Georgia, Kenneth McGarity finally received his Purple Heart, an Air Medal, and four additional prestigious awards.
3. Theresa and the girls returned home to stay in 1992. As a family, they worked through the anger and pain each of them had to deal with, and by the following year the McGaritys were doing well.

CHAPTER 8
WHATEVER HAPPENED TO HUMAN LIFE?

1. Joycelyn Elders, former surgeon general, accused pro-lifers of carrying on a "love affair with the fetus" at an abortion rights rally in January 1992.

2. Medieval philosophers had argued from the existence of God to the reality of the world. Descartes reversed that, and from then on philosophers argued from the certainty of the self to the reality of God and the world. From human reason alone, philosophers would discover all truth. This was the birth of the autonomy of human reason.

3. Friedrich Nietzsche, *The Gay Science*, trans. Walter Kaufmann (New York: Random, 1974), 125.

4. Peter Kreeft, "The World's Last Night," *Crisis* (July/August 1994): 39.

5. Robert P. George, "Why Integrity Matters," speech given at the National Prayer Breakfast, February 7, 1998. Professor George subjects naturalistic ideas about sexual morality to searching philosophical criticism in his new book *In Defense of Natural Law* (New York: Clarendon Press, 1998), chapters 8, 9, 15, 16.

6. *Roe v. Wade*, 410 US 113 (1973).

7. Nearly a decade earlier, two eminent pediatricians at Yale-New Haven Hospital had supported the parents' right to let their severely handicapped children die in such cases and suggested that doctors present the option if parents don't bring it up themselves. See Raymond S. Duff and A. G. M. Campbell, "Moral and Ethical Dilemmas in the Special-Care Nursery," *New England Journal of Medicine* 289, no. 17 (October 25, 1973): 890–94.

8. Richard A. Gross, Alan Cox, Ruth Tatyrek, Michael Polly, and William A. Barnes, "Early Management and Decision Making for the Treatment of Myelomeningocele," *Pediatrics* 72, no. 4 (October 4, 1983): 450–58.

9. Tucker Carlson, "Eugenics, American Style," *The Weekly Standard* 2, no. 12 (December 2, 1996): 20.

10. Nat Hentoff, "Abortion as Self-Defense," *Washington Post*, 1 February 1997.

11. Carlson, "Eugenics, American Style," 20.

12. Christopher Scanlan, "Elders: I'm Willing to Be a Lightning Rod," *Houston Chronicle*, 17 December 1992.

13. Carlson, "Eugenics, American Style," 20.

14. See C. Everett Koop, "Life and Death and the Handicapped Unborn," *Issues in Law & Medicine* 5, no. 1 (June 22, 1989): 101.

15. Steven Pinker, "Why They Kill Their Newborns," *New York Times*, 2 November 1997. See also Andrew Ferguson, "How Steven Pinker's Mind Works," *The Weekly Standard* (January 12, 1998): 16.

16. As quoted in Cal Thomas, "Who Cares about Living When the Good Times Are Rolling," *Naples Daily News*, 16 July 1998.

17. Eileen I. McDonagh, *Breaking the Abortion Deadlock: From Choice to Consent* (New York: Oxford University Press, 1996), 7.
18. *Planned Parenthood v. Casey*, 112 S Ct 2791 (1992).
19. *Compassion in Dying v. Washington*, 850 F Supp 1454 (WD Wash 1994).
20. This decision was handed down in 1997. Despite the Supreme Court's unanimity in reversing the Ninth Circuit Court's ruling, there are reasons for concern that some justices are biding their time, awaiting an opportunity to manufacture a right to assisted suicide akin to the abortion right in *Roe*. See Robert P. George, "The Supreme Court's 1997 Term," *First Things*, no. 77 (October 1997).
21. *Compassion in Dying v. Washington*, 79 F 3d 790 (9th Cir 1996).
22. Charles Colson and Russell Hittinger, "Private Liberty . . . Public Chaos," *Washington Times*, 22 April 1996. In 1991 a survey in the *New England Journal of Medicine* revealed that in the Netherlands as many as 1,000 patients had been euthanized annually without giving consent; and in 4,500 cases, excessive medication leading to death was given without patient consent. But a new study shows that these numbers vastly underrepresent the true extent of euthanasia practice there. A 1991 report published by the Dutch government said that in 1990 approximately 8,100 additional people were killed by their doctors by intentional overdose of morphine. In February 1999, a study in a British medical journal found that 59 percent of the deaths by either euthanasia or assisted suicide in the Netherlands go unreported. Wesley J. Smith, "Suicide Pays," *First Things* (June/July 1999): 14–16.
23. Tony Mauro, "Disabled Plan Protest against Assisted Suicide," *USA Today*, 6 January 1997.
24. Eric Zorn, "'Brave New World' Awaits Debaters of Abortion Rights," *Chicago Tribune*, 9 March 1997.
25. "Michael Has Four Parents: The Politics of Childbearing," *BreakPoint* commentary, June 21, 1995.
26. I strongly recommend reading Richard John Neuhaus, "The Return of Eugenics," *Commentary* (April 1988): 18–26.

CHAPTER 9
IN WHOSE IMAGE?

1. Steve Weizman, "Copenhagen Zoo Displays the Most Dangerous Animals," 12 September 1996, on-line Reuters North American Wire.
2. Ibid.

3. Mike Samuels and Nancy Samuels, as quoted in Robert D. Orr and Walter L. Larimore, "Medical Abortion Is Not Just a Medical Issue," *American Family Physician* 56, no. 2 (August 1997): 351.

4. Stanley Fish later disavowed much of what he said in Boston, or at least what most participants thought he said. Fish claimed that he has never been pro-choice, so what he said was no reversal of his position. He also claimed that he was not endorsing the pro-life position; he was merely acknowledging that he was mistaken in saying that pro-life arguments are religious, while pro-choice arguments are rational. In subsequent correspondence with me, he revealed the utterly self-refuting character of his own view. He argued that no moral position can be supported rationally—but of course he arrived at that position by thinking rationally. See also Stanley Fish, "Why Can't We All Get Along?" *First Things*, no. 60 (February 1996): 18.

5. C. S. Lewis, *Mere Christianity* (New York: Touchstone, 1996), 73.

6. Abraham Kuyper, *Christianity: A Total World and Life System* (Marlborough, N.H.: Plymouth Rock Foundation, 1996), 14.

7. See chapter 4 of Alvin J. Schmidt, *The Menace of Multiculturalism: Trojan Horse in America* (Westport, Conn.: Praeger, 1997).

8. Ted Turner, as quoted in Pat Buchanan, "Sermon from Ted Turner," *Washington Times*, 2 April 1997.

9. *The River*, Universal Pictures (1984).

10. Douglas Sadownick, "Choosing Sides," *LA Weekly*, 20 December 1996.

11. This is the same conflict Carl Sagan confronted when he was given the choice between certain death or submitting to a lifesaving treatment perfected through animal research (see chapter 6).

12. "A New Medical Ethics," *California Medicine* 113 (1970): 67–68.

13. A study done by Marv Miller shows that the inner state of emptiness among the elderly leads to an alarmingly high rate of suicide—especially older men after retirement (four times greater than the average rate for the U.S.). Marv Miller, *Suicide after Sixty: The Final Alternative* (New York: Springer, 1979), 11–12, 19.

14. Elizabeth Kolbert, "Frank Talk by Clinton to MTV Generation," *New York Times*, 20 April 1994.

15. Albert Camus, "Absurd Reasoning," *The Myth of Sisyphus*, trans. Justin O'Brien (New York: Alfred A. Knopf, 1969), 3.

16. Saint Augustine, *Confessions*, book 1, paragraph 1, trans. R. S. Pine-Coffin (New York: Penguin, 1961), 21.

RECOMMENDED READING

WORLDVIEW

Bellah, Robert. *The Good Society*. New York: Alfred A. Knopf, 1991.

Berger, Peter and Brigitte Berger, and Hansfried Kellner. *The Homeless Mind: Modernization and Consciousness*. New York: Random, 1974.

Blamires, Harry. *The Christian Mind*. Ann Arbor, Mich.: Servant, 1978.

Brown, Harold O. J. *The Sensate Culture*. Dallas: Word, 1996.

Carson, D. A., and John D. Woodbridge, eds. *God and Culture: Essays in Honor of Carl F. H. Henry*. Grand Rapids: Eerdmans, 1993.

Colson, Charles, with Anne Morse. *Burden of Truth: Defending Truth in an Age of Unbelief*. Wheaton, Ill.: Tyndale House, 1997.

Colson, Charles, with Nancy Pearcey. *A Dance with Deception: Revealing the Truth Behind the Headlines*. Dallas: Word, 1993.

Colson, Charles, with Ellen Santilli Vaughn. *The Body*. Dallas: Word, 1992.

Dawson, Christopher. *Religion and the Rise of Western Culture*. New York: Doubleday, 1991.

Dockery, David S., ed. *The Challenge of Postmodernism: An Evangelical Engagement*. Grand Rapids: Baker, 1997.

Dooyeweerd, Hermann. *Roots of Western Culture: Pagan, Secular, and Christian Options*. Toronto: Wedge, 1979.

———. *In the Twilight of Western Thought: Studies in the Pretended Autonomy of Philosophical Thought*. Lewiston, N.Y.: E. Mellen, 1999.

Eliot, T. S. *Christianity and Culture*. New York: Harcourt, Brace and Jovanovich, 1968.

Geisler, Norman L., and Ronald M. Brooks. *When Skeptics Ask: A Handbook of Christian Evidence*. Wheaton, Ill.: Victor, 1998.

Glover, Willis B. *Biblical Origins of Modern Secular Culture: An Essay in the Interpretation of Western History.* Macon, Ga.: Mercer University Press, 1984.

Grisez, Germain G. *The Way of the Lord Jesus.* Vol. 1, *Christian Moral Principles.* Chicago: Franciscan Herald Press, 1983.

———. *The Way of the Lord Jesus.* Vol. 2, *Living a Christian Life.* Quincy, Ill.: Franciscan Press, 1993.

———. *The Way of the Lord Jesus.* Vol. 3, *Difficult Moral Questions.* Quincy, Ill.: Franciscan Press, 1997.

Gunton, Colin. *Enlightenment and Alienation: An Essay Toward a Trinitarian Theology.* Grand Rapids: Eerdmans, 1985.

Halton, Eugene. *Bereft of Reason: On the Decline of Social Thought and Prospects for Its Renewal.* Chicago: University of Chicago Press, 1995.

Henry, Carl F. H. *The Christian Mind-set in a Secular Society: Promoting Evangelical Renewal and National Righteousness.* Portland, Ore.: Multnomah, 1978.

Heslam, Peter S. *Creating a Christian Worldview: Abraham Kuyper's Lectures on Calvinism.* Grand Rapids: Eerdmans, 1998.

Hoffecker, W. Andrew, and Gary Scott Smith, eds. *Building a Christian Worldview.* Vol. 1, *God, Man, and Knowledge.* Phillipsburg, N.J.: Presbyterian and Reformed, 1986.

Holmes, Arthur. *All Truth Is God's Truth.* Grand Rapids: Eerdmans, 1977.

Holmes, Arthur, ed. *The Making of a Christian Mind: A Christian World View & the Academic Enterprise.* Downers Grove, Ill.: InterVarsity Press, 1985.

Kuyper, Abraham. *Christianity: A Total World and Life System.* Marlborough, N.H.: Plymouth Rock Foundation, 1996.

Machen, J. Gresham. *Christianity and Liberalism.* Grand Rapids: Eerdmans, 1990.

Moreland, J. P. *Love Your God with All Your Mind: The Role of Reason in the Life of the Soul.* Colorado Springs: NavPress, 1997.

Noll, Mark. *The Scandal of the Evangelical Mind.* Downers Grove, Ill.: InterVarsity Press, 1994.

Runner, H. Evan. *The Relation of the Bible to Learning.* Toronto: Wedge, 1970.

Schaeffer, Francis. *The Complete Works of Francis A. Schaeffer: A Christian Worldview.* Westchester, Ill.: Crossway, 1982.

————. *25 Basic Bible Studies: Including Two Contents, Two Realities.* Wheaton, Ill.: Crossway, 1996. Also in *The Complete Works of Francis A. Schaeffer: A Christian Worldview.* Vol. 3, *A Christian View of Spirituality.* Westchester, Ill.: Crossway, 1982.

————. *Art and the Bible.* Downers Grove, Ill.: InterVarsity Press, 1973. Also in *The Complete Works of Francis A. Schaeffer: A Christian Worldview.* Vol. 2, *A Christian View of the Bible as Truth.* Westchester, Ill.: Crossway, 1982.

————. *Back to Freedom and Dignity.* In *The Complete Works of Francis A. Schaeffer: A Christian Worldview.* Vol. 1, *A Christian View of Philosophy and Culture.* Westchester, Ill.: Crossway, 1982.

————. *Basic Bible Studies.* In *The Complete Works of Francis A. Schaeffer: A Christian Worldview.* Vol. 2, *A Christian View of the Bible as Truth.* Westchester, Ill.: Crossway, 1982.

————. *A Christian Manifesto.* Wheaton, Ill.: Good News, 1982. Also in *The Complete Works of Francis A. Schaeffer: A Christian Worldview.* Vol. 5, *A Christian View of the West.* Westchester, Ill.: Crossway, 1982.

————. *The Church at the End of the Twentieth Century: Including, the Church Before the Watching World.* Wheaton, Ill.: Crossway, 1994.

————. *Death in the City.* In *The Complete Works of Francis A. Schaeffer: A Christian Worldview.* Vol. 4, *A Christian View of the Church.* Westchester, Ill.: Crossway, 1982.

————. *Genesis in Space and Time.* Downers Grove, Ill.: InterVarsity Press, 1972.

————. *The Great Evangelical Disaster.* Wheaton, Ill.: Good News, 1984.

————. *He Is There and He Is Not Silent.* Wheaton, Ill.: Tyndale House, 1972. Also in *The Complete Works of Francis A. Schaeffer: A Christian Worldview.* Vol. 1, *A Christian View of Philosophy and Culture.* Westchester, Ill.: Crossway, 1982.

————. *How Should We Then Live?* Westchester, Ill.: Crossway, 1983. Also in *The Complete Works of Francis A. Schaeffer: A Christian Worldview.* Vol. 5, *A Christian View of the West.* Westchester, Ill.: Crossway, 1982.

————. *Joshua and the Flow of Biblical History.* In *The Complete Works of Francis A. Schaeffer: A Christian Worldview.* Vol. 2, *A Christian View of the Bible as Truth.* Westchester, Ill.: Crossway, 1982.

————. *The Mark of the Christian*. In *The Complete Works of Francis A. Schaeffer: A Christian Worldview*. Vol. 4, *A Christian View of the Church*. Westchester, Ill.: Crossway, 1982.

————. *The New Super-Spirituality*. In *The Complete Works of Francis A. Schaeffer: A Christian Worldview*. Vol. 3, *A Christian View of Spirituality*. Westchester, Ill.: Crossway, 1982.

————. *No Final Conflict*. In *The Complete Works of Francis A. Schaeffer: A Christian Worldview*. Vol. 2, *A Christian View of the Bible as Truth*. Westchester, Ill.: Crossway, 1982.

————. *No Little People*. In *The Complete Works of Francis A. Schaeffer: A Christian Worldview*. Vol. 3, *A Christian View of Spirituality*. Westchester, Ill.: Crossway, 1982.

————. *True Spirituality*. Wheaton, Ill.: Tyndale House, 1979. Also in *The Complete Works of Francis A. Schaeffer: A Christian Worldview*. Vol. 3, *A Christian View of Spirituality*. Westchester, Ill.: Crossway, 1982.

Schaeffer, Francis A., and C. Everett Koop. *Whatever Happened to the Human Race?* Westchester, Ill.: Crossway, 1983. Also in *The Complete Works of Francis A. Schaeffer: A Christian Worldview*. Vol. 5, *A Christian View of the West*. Westchester, Ill.: Crossway, 1982.

Schaeffer, Francis A., and Udo Middelmann. *Pollution and the Death of Man*. Wheaton, Ill.: Crossway, 1992. Also in *The Complete Works of Francis A. Schaeffer: A Christian Worldview*. Vol. 5, *A Christian View of the West*. Westchester, Ill.: Crossway, 1982.

Sire, James W. *The Universe Next Door: A Basic Worldview Catalog*. 3rd ed. Downers Grove, Ill.: InterVarsity Press, 1997.

Smart, Ninian. *Worldviews: Crosscultural Explorations of Human Beliefs*. 2nd ed. Englewood Cliffs, N.J.: Prentice Hall, 1995.

Sorokin, Pitirim A. *The Crisis of Our Age*. 2nd rev. ed. London: Oneworld, 1992.

Sproul, R. C. *Lifeviews*. Grand Rapids: Baker, 1990.

Vander Goot, Henry. *Life Is Religion: Essays in Honor of H. Evan Runner*. St. Catherines, Ontario: Paideia, 1981.

Veith, Gene Edward. *Postmodern Times: A Christian Guide to Contemporary Thought and Culture*. Wheaton, Ill.: Crossway, 1994.

Walsh, Brian J., and J. Richard Middleton. *The Transforming Vision: Shaping a Christian World View*. Downers Grove, Ill.: InterVarsity Press, 1984.

Wells, David F. *No Place for Truth, or, Whatever Happened to Evangelical Theology?* Grand Rapids: Eerdmans, 1993.

Wolters, Albert M. *Creation Regained: Biblical Basics for a Reformational Worldview.* Grand Rapids: Eerdmans, 1985.

CREATION

Aeschliman, Michael D. *The Restitution of Man: C. S. Lewis and the Case against Scientism.* Grand Rapids: Eerdmans, 1983.

Behe, Michael. *Darwin's Black Box: The Biochemical Challenge to Evolution.* New York: Touchstone, 1996.

Corey, M. A. *God and the New Cosmology: The Anthropic Design Argument.* Lanham, Md.: Rowman & Littlefield, 1993.

Craig, William Lane, and Quentin Smith. *Theism, Atheism, and Big Bang Cosmology.* New York: Oxford University Press, 1993.

Davis, Percival, and Dean Kenyon. *Of Pandas and People: The Central Question of Biological Origins.* 2nd ed. Dallas: Haughton, 1993.

Dembski, William A. *The Design Inference: Eliminating Chance through Small Probabilities.* Cambridge: Cambridge University Press, 1998.

Dembski, William A., ed. *Mere Creation: Science, Faith, and Intelligent Design.* Downers Grove, Ill.: InterVarsity Press, 1998.

Denton, Michael. *Evolution: A Theory in Crisis.* Bethesda, Md.: Adler & Adler, 1985.

Johnson, Phillip E. *Darwin on Trial.* 2nd ed. Downers Grove, Ill.: InterVarsity Press, 1993.

――――. *Defeating Darwinism: By Opening Minds.* Downers Grove, Ill.: InterVarsity Press, 1997.

――――. *Objections Sustained: Subversive Essays on Evolution, Law, and Culture.* Downers Grove, Ill.: InterVarsity Press, 1998.

――――. *Reason in the Balance: The Case against Naturalism in Science, Law, and Education.* Downers Grove, Ill.: InterVarsity Press, 1995.

Macbeth, Norman. *Darwin Retried.* New York: Delta Books, 1971.

Moreland, J. P. *Christianity and the Nature of Science.* Grand Rapids: Baker, 1990.

Overman, Dean. *The Case against Accident and Self-Organization.* New York: Rowman and Littlefield, 1997.

Pearcey, Nancy R., and Charles B. Thaxton. *The Soul of Science: Christian Faith and Natural Philosophy.* Wheaton, Ill.: Crossway, 1994.

Polanyi, Michael. *Science, Faith and Society.* Chicago: University of Chicago Press, 1964.

Thaxton, Charles B., Walter Bradley, and Roger Olsen. *The Mystery of Life's Origin: Reassessing Current Theories.* Dallas: Lewis and Stanley, 1992.

ABOUT THE AUTHORS

Charles W. Colson graduated with honors from Brown University and received his Juris Doctor from George Washington University. From 1969 to 1973 he served as special counsel to President Richard Nixon. In 1974 he pleaded guilty to charges related to Watergate and served seven months in a federal prison.

Before going to prison, Charles Colson was converted to Christ, as told in *Born Again*. He has also published *Life Sentence, Crime and the Responsible Community, Convicted* (with Dan Van Ness), *How Now Shall We Live?* (with Nancy Pearcey), *The Body* (with Ellen Vaughn), *A Dance with Deception* (with Nancy Pearcey), *A Dangerous Grace* (with Nancy Pearcey), *Gideon's Torch* (with Ellen Vaughn), *Burden of Truth* (with Anne Morse), *The God of Stones and Spiders, Why America Doesn't Work* (with Jack Eckerd), *Answers to Your Kids' Questions* (with Harold Fickett), *Who Speaks for God?, Kingdoms in Conflict, Against the Night,* and *Loving God,* the book many people consider to be a contemporary classic.

Colson founded Prison Fellowship Ministries (PF), an interdenominational outreach, now active in eighty-eight countries. The world's largest prison ministry, PF manages over 50,000 active volunteers in the U.S. and tens of thousands more abroad. The ministry provides Bible studies in more than 1,000 prisons, conducts over 2,000 in-prison seminars per year, does major evangelistic outreaches, and reaches more than 500,000 kids at Christmas with gifts and the love of Christ. The ministry also has two subsidiaries: Justice Fellowship, which works for biblically based criminal justice policies, and Neighbors Who Care, a network of volunteers providing assistance to victims of crime. Also a part of the ministry is the Wilberforce Forum, which provides worldview materials for the Christian community, including Colson's daily radio broadcast, *BreakPoint*, now heard on a thousand outlets.

Colson has received fifteen honorary doctorates and in 1993 was awarded the Templeton Prize, the world's largest cash gift (over $1 million), which is given each year to the one person in the world who has done the most to advance the cause of religion. Colson donated this prize, as he does all speaking fees and royalties, to further the work of PF.

■　　■　　■

Nancy R. Pearcey studied under Francis Schaeffer at L'Abri Fellowship in Switzerland in 1971 and 1972 and then earned a master's degree from Covenant Theological Seminary and did graduate work at the Institute for Christian Studies in Toronto. She is coauthor with Charles Thaxton of the book *The Soul of Science: Christian Faith and Natural Philosophy* and has contributed chapters to several other books, including *Mere Creation, Of Pandas and People,* and *Pro-Life Feminism.* Her articles have appeared in journals and magazines such as *First Things, Books and Culture, The World & I, The Family in America,* and *The Human Life Review.*

Pearcey is currently a fellow with the Discovery Institute's Center for the Renewal for Science and Culture, in Seattle, and managing editor of the journal *Origins and Design.* She is policy director of the Wilberforce Forum and executive editor of Colson's *BreakPoint,* a daily radio commentary program that analyzes current issues from a Christian worldview perspective. She is also coauthor with Colson of a monthly column in *Christianity Today.*

HOW NOW SHALL WE LIVE?

helps Christians make sense of the competing worldviews that clamor for attention and allegiance in a pluralistic society. Pulling no punches, Colson and Pearcey show that all other worldviews fail to meet the test of rational consistency or practical application in the real world. Only the Christian worldview provides a rationally sustainable way to understand the universe. Only the Christian worldview fits the real world and can be lived out consistently in every area of life.

Weaving together engaging stories with penetrating analysis of ideas, *How Now Shall We Live?* helps Christians defend their faith and live out its full implications in every arena—the home, workplace, classroom, courtroom, and public policy. It is a defining book for Christians in this new millennium.

Resources available from Tyndale House Publishers that support the message and ministry of *How Now Shall We Live?*

How Now Shall We Live?: cloth

How Now Shall We Live? Study Guide: paper
Two thirteen-week Bible lessons to help Bible study groups absorb and apply the concepts of Colson's magnum opus

How Now Shall We Live? Audio Book: The abridged version on four audiocassettes

Answers to Your Kids' Questions: A guide to help parents know how to talk to their kids about the worldview issues they face every day

Complete adult and youth video curriculum is available from LifeWay Church Resources.

Order by writing to LifeWay Church Resources Customer Service, MSN 113, 127 Ninth Avenue North, Nashville, TN 37211-0113; by calling toll free (800) 458-2772; by faxing (615) 251-5933; or by e-mailing customerservice@lifeway.com.

Look for other books and materials based on *How Now Shall We Live?* from Tyndale House Publishers.

Visit these Web sites for more information:

Charles Colson's books and tapes: chuckcolson.com

Breakpoint: breakpoint.org

Prison Fellowship Ministries: pfm.org

Other books by Tyndale House Publishers: tyndale.com

Addresses for more information:

Terry White
Communications Department
Prison Fellowship Ministries
P.O. Box 17500
Washington, DC 20041-0500

Public Relations
Tyndale House Publishers, Inc.
351 Executive Drive
Carol Stream, IL 60188
phone: (630) 668-8300
fax: (630) 668-3245

The content of this series is drawn from the major sections of *How Now Shall We Live?* Shorter in length, more acessible to readers, and with added questions, these books are ideal for group study. Each book will help readers engage Colson's ideas and learn how to apply them to the world around them.

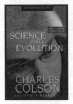 *Developing a Christian Worldview of Science and Evolution:* paper

 *Developing a Christian Worldview of the Problem of Evil:* paper

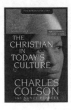 *Developing a Christian Worldview of the Christian in Today's Culture:* paper